T0319071

The Marriage of Maria Braun

German Film Classics

Series Editors
Gerd Gemünden, Dartmouth College
Johannes von Moltke, University of Michigan

Advising Editors
Anton Kaes, University of California-Berkeley
Eric Rentschler, Harvard University

Editorial Board
Hester Baer, University of Maryland
Mattias Frey, University of Kent
Rembert Hüser, Goethe University, Frankfurt
Cristina Nord, Berlinale Forum
Brad Prager, University of Missouri
Reinhild Steingröver, Eastman School of Music

Also in the series:

THE MARRIAGE OF MARIA BRAUN

PRISCILLA LAYNE

 CAMDEN HOUSE

First published 2024 by Camden House

Camden House is an imprint of Boydell & Brewer Inc.
668 Mt. Hope Avenue, Rochester, NY 14620, USA
and of Boydell & Brewer Limited
PO Box 9, Woodbridge, Suffolk IP12 3DF, UK
www.boydellandbrewer.com

Cover image: Scene from *The Marriage of Maria Braun.* Used by permission of DFF – Deutsches Filminstitut & Filmmuseum, Frankfurt am Main / Fassbinder Collection. Permanent loan of Rainer Werner Fassbinder Foundation © RWFF.

ISBN-13: 978-1-57113-504-9

Library of Congress Cataloging-in-Publication Data
CIP data is available from the Library of Congress.

CONTENTS

The Marriage of Maria Braun

About midway through the film *The Marriage of Maria Braun*, director Rainer Werner Fassbinder's title character sees an opportunity to improve her socioeconomic situation, and she sets everything in motion to seize it. The setting is postwar Germany in the American-occupied sector and Maria, a presumed widow, is hoping to get a job working at an illegal bar that caters to African American soldiers. The bar owner, a shady character by the name of Bronski, dissuades her, telling her "We don't need anybody." Maria's reply demonstrates the beaming confidence that will carry her through the rest of the film: "Maybe once you've got me you won't need anybody else." This scene is similar to an equally life-changing moment in one of the many films that inspired *Maria Braun*, the German émigré Douglas Sirk's melodrama *Imitation of Life* (1959). In Sirk's film, the lead character is also a widow, Lora—a sultry blonde played by Lana Turner. Like Maria Braun, Lora is also trying to fake it until she makes it. An aspiring actress, Lora tries to fool a talent agent, Allen Loomis, into casting her in a role. What allows Lora to fake the qualifications for the job is her quick thinking, fast talking, and, most importantly, a Black woman named Annie, whose presence in Lora's life convinces others that Lora *must* be successful; how else could she afford to employ a maid?

What Maria Braun and Lora have in common are a similar attitude towards surviving in a world that is not meant for independent women. Both are living as widows, trying to scrape by financially. Lora has the added burden of a child, while Maria helps support her mother, with whom she lives. Furthermore, from a critical perspective on race and gender, although Maria Braun and Lora use their gumption to get their foot inside the door, they must also use their relationships with Black people to get ahead, while being willing to callously throw these Black people aside when it suits them. In reality, Lora is making ends meet, doing small parts in commercials. And Annie is not actually being paid to work as Lora's maid but is (like Lora) a single mother, who has made a deal with her: in exchange for a place for Annie and her daughter, Sarah Jane, to live, Annie will work as a maid and watch Lora's daughter, Susie. Annie's hypervisible, racialized domestic labor, and her invisible friendship, give Lora both the support she needs to work outside the home getting acting jobs, and the appearance of being wealthy enough that people are willing to give her credit and assume she is a successful actress. Lora supposes that she and Annie are equals, friends even. It takes Sarah Jane to point out that Lora doesn't actually treat Annie like a friend. In fact, when Lora has her friends over, she expects Annie *and* Sarah Jane to *serve* them, precisely because they are Black. Throughout the film, Lora doesn't realize how little she knows about Annie's life, until the day of Annie's funeral when Black Americans turn up in droves to honor her; a scene that Fassbinder found so significant that he mentioned it twice in his short essay "Six Films by Douglas Sirk." Fassbinder writes:

> Annie doesn't want a spectacular funeral because she'd get anything out of it, she's dead by then, but because she wants to give herself value in the eyes of the world retrospectively, which she was denied during her lifetime. . . . Then they [Lora, Sarah Jane, and Susie] all come together again at Annie's funeral, and behave for a few minutes as though everything was all right. It's this "as though" that lets them carry on with the same old crap, underneath they have an inkling of what they are really after, but they soon forget it again.[1]

Fassbinder's discussion of this scene demonstrates why he found it such a perfect encapsulation of two psychological issues that also concerned him in *Maria Braun*: first, why are people willing to defer their happiness until it's too late? And second, why is it so difficult for people to actually *change* the world, even if they can identify what's wrong with it? Lora is aware of the racism at work in society that structurally separates her from Annie's life, but she'd rather not actually do anything about it. She looks at Sarah Jane as a tragic figure, while expecting her and Annie to serve her dinner guests without protest. Fassbinder recognizes the hypocrisy of Lora's behavior. He notes how she is "baffled" that Annie had *any* friends, let alone the number of people who came to her funeral: "The two women had been living together under one roof for ten years by then, and Lana [Lora] knows nothing about Annie. No wonder Lana Turner is surprised."[2] As long as Lora could continue pretending that she and Annie were friends, she never had to actually scrutinize her own behavior and privilege.

Maria Braun has similarly callous attitudes towards the Black *men* she encounters during the American occupation of West Germany. Her relationship with the African American GI Bill helps her survive the immediate postwar years. He teaches her English and provides her with goods until her German husband, Hermann, whom she thought was dead, returns home. When Hermann appears at her door, she not only tosses Bill aside, but murders him, choosing to rehabilitate Hermann's injured masculinity instead. And even though she must live the next several decades without her husband, who goes to jail after confessing to the murder in her place, Maria continues to thrive in part *because* of her proximity to Black men. The English that Bill taught her helps her land a job with a French German industrialist named Oswald. And what helps her impress Oswald is how she can use English to masterfully negotiate an awkward situation with a drunk Black GI she encounters on a train.

The reason I begin with this comparison between *Maria Braun* and Sirk's *Imitation of Life* is that the two films are connected by several key themes, including how they center a white heroine who is suffering under the weight of society—forces like sexism and patriarchy that make it difficult for her to succeed. For example, when Loomis catches on to Lora's ruse and exposes her, he offers her a deal: he will make her a star, but she has to be available for him in every way, including for sexual favors. But while Lora, the moral female character of Sirk's melodrama, adamantly rejects this proposition, Maria Braun is a different kind of character entirely. She leans *into* the moral danger that comes with working as an *Animierdame* (or "bar girl"). Bronski does warn her, but, as we keep learning throughout the film, Maria is willing to do whatever it takes to survive her difficult economic circumstances. Fassbinder has no intention of delivering a classical Hollywood melodrama, a genre Thomas Schatz describes as being defined by its "virtuous, long-suffering heroines whose persistent faith in the American Dream [is] finally rewarded with romantic love and a house in the suburbs."[3] Rather, *Maria Braun* may start with a wedding, but the sought-after "romantic love and a house in the suburbs" go up in smoke in a climactic explosion at the end of the film. What Lora and Maria *do*, however, have in common is that they are both working-class white women attempting to climb the social ladder, and that their economic success depends in part on their using and discarding Black people.

On the surface, Maria Braun's story may lead us to believe that she is an antihero we should be rooting for. The film opens with her wedding to Hermann Braun, a soldier in the German Army who subsequently returns to the fighting on the Eastern Front. Although the film begins with the wedding in 1943, we transition immediately after the opening credits to two years later. Maria is sharing a dilapidated apartment with her mother, her friend Betti, and her mother's boyfriend, Grandpa Berger. Maria fears Hermann may be dead or in a POW camp. When she hears from a fellow soldier that he is in fact dead, she attempts to move on, getting a job in the local bar catering to African American soldiers. There she meets and falls in love with Bill, a Black GI, who takes good care of her and her family. However, when Maria discovers that she is pregnant, and she and Bill attempt to celebrate the good news by having sex, they are caught *in flagrante* by her husband, who is alive and has returned from the front after all. Up until this point, one could characterize Maria as simply a practical woman, like many German women after the war, who is doing what she must to survive. Once Hermann has returned, however, rather than either choosing her new lover Bill, or alternatively simply ending things with him and going back to Hermann, she kills Bill on the spot. Fassbinder's message is that when given the choice between following a new path (represented by Bill) or falling into an old pattern (represented by Hermann), Maria, as a representative for Germany, will stick with the status quo rather than attempting to change the system.

This is the pattern Maria Braun's life follows throughout the rest of the film. After Hermann sacrifices himself, going to jail for Bill's murder, she moves south and begins working for the aforementioned Karl Oswald, who is in the business of manufacturing stockings—a hot commodity that is hard to come by in the early postwar period. In Oswald's company, Maria works her way up from secretary to business partner, all while trying to keep her romantic dealings with Oswald separate from their business relationship. Maria believes that she is smart enough to work the system of sexism and patriarchy to her advantage, if she just remains in control. She decides whether and when she and Oswald have sex or simply spend time together. She doesn't want to accept gifts from him. She doesn't want to marry him or blur the lines between their professional and personal relationships. She believes that if her relationship with Oswald remains transactional, she can have it all: inherit Oswald's money when he dies, be reunited with her husband when he leaves jail, and provide them both with a comfortable lifestyle. However, these plans are foiled in the end when Maria learns that even though she had kept Oswald in the dark about Hermann and tried to keep the two men apart from each other, Oswald and Hermann had actually made a deal behind her back regarding ownership over her, denying her agency. Oswald secretly follows Maria on one of the occasions she visits Hermann in jail. And, unbeknownst to her, Oswald offers to give Hermann half of his inheritance if Hermann agrees to stay out of their relationship until Oswald is dead. Thus, while Maria was toiling away, doing everything in her power to *reunite* with Hermann, Oswald used his power and money to keep Hermann away. After being confronted with her marginalization and lack of power as a woman, Maria tragically dies in her villa, along with Hermann, due to a gas explosion, which may have been suicide or just an accident. In his own remarks, Fassbinder connects Maria's disillusionment over her treatment at the hands of these men in her life with a general recognition that the Federal Republic of Germany (FRG, aka West Germany) could never live up to its ideals:

> Sure, she learns man stuff; she learns how to deal with the traders on the black market. She learns the tricks that are necessary as a survival technique in the first postwar years. She also quickly understands that if you want to be successful, you have to stick to the prevailing will to rebuild in the Federal Republic. But she doesn't invest in her feelings, or her whole person. She only seems to see that the necessity she learned from the war to survive must now seamlessly transition to the need to become wealthy no matter what. . . . It is often said that . . . at the beginning of this republic so much value was placed on amassing material goods and that that's to blame for the spiritual impoverishment of the society that supports the state. The state in which Maria Braun would have wanted to live would certainly have looked different. In it—for example—a contract between men about the disposal of a woman's life years would not have been possible. But that was not the state that the Federal Republic became.[4]

Rising from the Ashes

In 1979, the Federal Republic was having to reckon with political extremes from different directions. On the one hand, the country was still working through its fascist past. In January of that year, the public television station ARD began screening the four-part American miniseries *Holocaust* (1978), which started a whole new debate about Germany's *Vergangenheitsbewältigung* (coming to terms with the past). In July, the West German parliament rescinded the statute of limitations for murder, so that newly discovered Nazi crimes could still be prosecuted. And in September, the Federal Supreme Court ruled that it was libel to deny the fact that millions of Jews had been murdered by the Nazis.

On the other hand, West Germany was also facing political difficulties in the present. In January, the left-wing terrorist Irmgard Möller, a former member of the Red Army Faction terrorist group (RAF, also known as the Baader-Meinhof Gang), was sentenced to life in prison for murder and attempted murder. That same month, the local government of the city of Hamburg ruled that a teacher who was a member of the Communist Party could no longer be banned from civil service. In February, the former RAF lawyer Klaus Croissant was sentenced to two and a half years of jail and a four-year occupational ban for supporting a criminal organization. And in December, Rudi Dutschke, who had been a leader of the 1968 student movement, died due to the long-term effects of an assassination attempt eleven years earlier.

Considering this context, it is no wonder that in the very same year, two groundbreaking films were released that contributed to working through the past and interrogating the continuities between Nazi Germany and the Federal Republic: Völker Schlöndorff's adaptation of Günter Grass's novel *The Tin Drum* and Fassbinder's film *The Marriage of Maria Braun*.

Maria Braun had its premiere at the Berlinale, the Berlin Film Festival, on February 20, 1979. Prior to this, Fassbinder had held a private screening of it for film critics—on May 22, 1978—after his previous film, *Despair*, was snubbed at Cannes. Though Fassbinder didn't win the Golden Bear for best film at the Berlinale, *Maria Braun* would go on to win a Bambi Award for Best Film, which is the German equivalent of an Academy Award—the national media prize of the Federal Republic. This recognition was in large part because *Maria Braun* was considered Fassbinder's most accessible, most commercial, and most mature work.[5] What made the film stand out was that in a climate where the average moviegoer was alienated by and disinterested in the other arthouse films of New German Cinema, preferring instead to see dubbed Hollywood movies, *Maria Braun* actually attracted a lot of German viewers. In its first year alone, half a million viewers watched it and it grossed three million marks (the equivalent to over a million dollars). In 1980, *Maria Braun* was ranked fourteenth among domestic films at the German box office. The only arthouse film that was more popular was Schlöndorff's *The Tin Drum*, in fifth place.

Fassbinder is known for his tendency to center the stories of marginalized people who can't help but cling to the very system, or person, that is actively oppressing them. His obsession with the inner workings of power and oppression left its mark on all forty-three of his films, regardless of the protagonists' gender, race, or sexuality. In *Whity* (1971), an enslaved Black man has a hard time rebelling against the white family that has been abusing him his entire life. In *The Bitter Tears of Petra van Kant* (1972), we witness the white German fashion designer Petra becoming infatuated with her younger, white female lover, Karin, who in turn does anything and everything to make her jealous. In *Ali: Fear Eats the Soul* (1974), the Moroccan guest worker Ali seeks solace from Germany's racist society in the arms of white, female lovers who often dehumanize him, seeing him as solely a romantic companion and nothing else.

And in *In a Year with 13 Moons* (1978), Elvira, who was once the burly white German working-class butcher Erwin, tries desperately to keep her boyfriend happy, even undergoing gender reassignment surgery, only for him to abandon her. But despite the commonalities shared across these characters, it is without a doubt Maria Braun who is Fassbinder's most famous antihero.

Maria Braun was the first installment of Fassbinder's "BRD trilogy"—a retelling, through the lives of three female protagonists, of the founding years of the Federal Republic. The subsequent films in the trilogy were *Lola* (1981) and *The Longing of Veronika Voss* (1982). This choice of female protagonists is no coincidence; from his first feature film, *Katzelmacher* (1969), to the "chamber play" *The Bitter Tears of Petra von Kant* and his adaptation of Fontane's *Effi Briest* (1974), Fassbinder had always been interested in the psychology of women: how they oppress others and are oppressed themselves. Once, when asked why women were so frequently the focus of his films, Fassbinder responded: "Every narrative is better when told about women. Men usually behave as society expects them to do. Women tend to swim against the norms. You [men] are more consistent, more transparent. Men always play their roles."[6]

In Maria Braun, we have a character who is precisely the opposite of such consistency, able to shapeshift and reinvent herself however necessary in order to survive, which is why she sarcastically calls herself the "Mata Hari of the economic miracle"—a reference to the early-twentieth-century white Dutch exotic dancer who reinvented herself as a Javanese princess of Indian descent. But many women in history have had to reinvent themselves to survive. Why would Fassbinder draw this particular comparison between Maria Braun, a white German woman presumed to be a war widow at the conclusion of World War II, and the Dutch dancer masquerading as a princess? What Mata Hari and Maria Braun have in common is a shared positionality (they are both white, heterosexual European women) and a common strategy: using their positionality to their best advantage in order to gain the most benefits, even while operating within a racist, sexist, and patriarchal system.

Although Fassbinder, together with Kurt Raab, had written an exposé on which the story of *Maria Braun* is loosely based, the actual script was written by Peter Märthesheimer, who at the time was an editor for the radio station WDR (Westdeutscher Rundfunk, or West German Radio). Fassbinder didn't write the script himself because at the time he was working on the script for his fifteen-hour epic television adaptation of Alfred Döblin's novel *Berlin Alexanderplatz* (1929), which was televised between October and December 1980. But Fassbinder made some changes to *Maria Braun's* shooting script, including to the film's ending. In the shooting script, after Hermann and Maria reunite, they go on a honeymoon trip together. Afterwards, they are both present for the reading of Oswald's will at a notary's office. In the will, Oswald had written, "I gave him [Hermann] the chance for independence. He gave me the chance for happiness," revealing the pact between them.[7] In the final scene, Maria and Hermann die in a murder/suicide as she intentionally drives them both over an embankment.

By changing this intentional car accident to a gas explosion, a much more ambiguous death, Fassbinder left audiences questioning whether or not the explosion was intended,[8] an ambivalence that more accurately reflected how Fassbinder wanted to depict Maria's mindset. If she intentionally kills Hermann and herself, it is because she refuses to live a life she cannot control. But if the explosion is an accident, brought about by her poor mental state after realizing the men in her life have deceived her, then her death is the kind of tragedy that happens when a woman attempts to gain control within a heteropatriarchal system. What Fassbinder attempted to achieve with this tale was to demonstrate that Maria's focus on her individual success is her downfall. She has several chances to undermine the status quo and join other marginalized people in solidarity, particularly when she has the choice of choosing Bill over

Hermann. But rather than trying to change the hegemonic system, she chooses instead to try to use it to her advantage, only to discover that this traps her in a vicious cycle of oppression that requires the marginalization of anyone who departs from the white male norm.

In the past, critics have debated many potential reasons why Maria must fail. For example, Peter Jansen, writing for *Die Zeit*, claims that by having Maria fail Fassbinder shows how difficult it can be for real women to "live this different kind of life;" namely a life of emancipation.[9] Taking a psychoanalytic approach, Ruth McCormick suggests that Maria fails because she (and Germany) need to fulfill their need for a father (a leader).[10] But what if Maria fails *not* because she attempts to break with the status quo, but precisely because of her complicity with it? In my analysis of the film, I will demonstrate how Maria is complicit with both the racism and the white patriarchy of the FRG. What differentiates my reading of Maria from McCormick's is rather than taking a psychoanalytic approach, I will draw on critical race theory, Black feminist thought, and critical whiteness studies to expand on the role of race and gender in the film and contextualize Fassbinder's portrayal of Black masculinity within his fetishization of Black men throughout his career. In addition to these topics, I will also look more closely at some of the intertexts Fassbinder uses in the film, especially Sirk's films, because of how they relate to his use of melodrama. Melodrama is an important part of how Fassbinder introduces conflicts along gendered and racialized lines, and in order to understand this, one has to be familiar with the melodramatic intertexts on which Fassbinder draws. Fassbinder once said that *Maria Braun* "is a wild, cruel, tender, inhuman—thus very human— story. In short, a melodrama. And melodramas, I'm sure, are film's only way of making despair tangible and experienceable."[11] Along with Sirk's films, an additional intertext on which Fassbinder draws is Carl Fröhlich's film *Es war eine rauschende Ballnacht* (It Was a Gay Ball Night, 1939). Fröhlich's film addresses the interaction of gender and power, and understanding Fassbinder's citation of it helps one further grasp *Maria Braun*'s arguments about German society.

Race and Gender in Postwar German Society

In order to understand how racism and sexism intersect in *Maria Braun*, one first needs an understanding of sex and race in the newly founded FRG, and of how Fassbinder's upbringing may have affected his art. No doubt, Fassbinder's interest in the themes of power, oppression, and exploitation stemmed from his life experiences: first, growing up as a gay man in the very conservative, Catholic, homophobic, and sexually repressive society of Bavaria, and second, growing up with a very independent and often cold woman, his mother Liselotte.

1950s West Germany is typically described as a conservative place and time, when West Germans desired to reestablish gender relations that reflected neither Nazi nor communist ideology. For West Germany, the East served as a useful foil against which the West could create an opposing identity. In East Germany, the government implemented policies that would create more gender equality, such as equal pay and equal access to education and employment opportunities. Furthermore, in the East *all* women, including married women and women with children, were encouraged to work full-time. To make this possible, the GDR had an extensive infrastructure of full-time state childcare. The conservative Christian West German government viewed these communist gender relations in the East as forcibly doing away with a natural difference between the sexes; in West Germany, by contrast, the government wished to "reconcile equality with difference" and establish a "'harmonious inequality' between women and men, especially in the endeavor to anchor the model of the so-called 'housewife marriage,' which was based on a breadwinner husband and a mother and housewife without (or with part-time) employment."[12] Hanna Schissler writes that "the men who returned from the front were frequently physically and mentally broken or otherwise seriously impaired," and the West German government was therefore interested in rehabilitating these men so that they could take their place as the rightful breadwinners.[13] This resulted in relatively conservative gender dynamics in the 1950s, during the era of Konrad Adenauer's chancellorship, a time when the West German government encouraged women to stay home and care for children. While the West German government's emphasis on women becoming stay-at-home mothers may be similar to the Nazis' attitudes towards women's place in society, as Dagmar Herzog points out in *Sex After Fascism*, Nazi Germany was not the conservative sexual regime people might assume it to have been. Herzog insists that Nazi sexual politics "coexisted with injunctions and encouragements to the majority of Germans to seek and experience sexual pleasure,"[14] including extramaritally. This is why, for example, the Nazi regime instituted brothels for its soldiers. Thus, rather than the FRG exhibiting a *continuation* of Nazi sexual politics, the West German state intentionally broke with this past and promoted more conservative and sexually repressive norms.

Fassbinder was born on May 31, 1945, just twenty-three days after World War II ended, in Bad Wörishofen, an hour west of Munich. Fassbinder claimed to remember hearing the bombs detonate from his mother's womb.[15] It is therefore no wonder that he grew up to be so obsessed with Nazi Germany and with West Germany's coming to terms with this past. Fassbinder suffered from the absence of both of his parents during his first year of life. This was another effect of the war. Fassbinder's parents were *Aussiedler* (resettlers), belonging to the millions of ethnic Germans who fled Eastern Europe following the war for fear of retaliation. These *Aussiedler* were not welcomed with open arms in occupied Germany. Instead, they were viewed as outsiders impinging on limited resources. During the first year of his life, Fassbinder was sent to live with relatives so that, without a baby to look after, both his parents could work and save money to find a better living situation.[16] The time that Fassbinder spent away from his mother during this formative time ultimately had a negative impact on their relationship. After they reunited, Liselotte found that she had a hard time bonding with him. Several other characteristics of Fassbinder's family also contributed to his feeling alienated, in addition to the fact that he had a working mother. First of all, his mother had been born in Central Poland and had a Slavic ethnic background, which contributed to the "exotic look" that critics ascribed to Fassbinder.[17] Secondly, his father, a doctor, often treated sex workers in his home practice. (In fact, his father eventually lost his medical license because he performed illegal abortions.) This may have been partly why Fassbinder was drawn to depicting the lives of outsiders in West Germany.

Interestingly, even after the Fassbinders moved into a larger, five-room apartment, they still had to share it with relatives, perhaps a result of the housing shortage following the war. And although Fassbinder's father worked as a doctor, his mother also continued to work, which was undoubtedly unusual at the time. This may be part of what led to Fassbinder's interest in female protagonists whose lives don't easily conform to gender conventions. Maria Braun, for instance, would not have been able to have the ideal "housewife marriage" promoted by the Christian Democrats in the 1950s. An assumed widow without any children, Maria was a perfect candidate for breaking away from the chains of domesticity following the war. If she had merely taken a white (male) lover—whether German, American, British, or French—she might have been able to maintain some form of respectability during the postwar period. However, by entering a relationship with an African American soldier, Maria moves further towards the margins of society.

The Americans may have been fighting for democracy in Germany, but they still occupied the country with a segregated army. And, as Timothy Schroer argues, that means they also brought a tradition of Jim Crow to Germany. White American soldiers preferred not to fraternize with their Black counterparts. Both white American and German men warned white German women to stay away from Black soldiers; some were even told that Black men had tails, because they were evolutionarily closer to monkeys. Nevertheless, as both Maria Höhn and Annette Brauerhoch find, some white German women still risked fraternizing with and engaging in relationships with Black GIs.[18] And as punishment, these women were condemned by society. It was often assumed that they were sex workers, because what white German woman would willingly have sex with a Black man if not for money? This stereotype is alluded to in *Maria Braun* when Maria seeks employment in the bar for Black GIs. The owner, Bronski, insists that she will have to get a clean bill of health from a doctor before she can start. The assumption is either that because she is willing to work in such a locale, she might possibly be a sex worker, *or* that working in such a locale requires that a woman be willing to have sexual relations with the customers.

There were more than a million African Americans serving in the US army at that time, but most Black soldiers were relegated to labor battalions, which meant that rather than fighting, they fulfilled domestic roles like cooking, cleaning, and logistics.[19] Thus, Black GIs had greater access to goods, and those goods were particularly desired by the starving German masses. One sees the segregated and inferior treatment of Black soldiers in Fassbinder's film, at the bar where Maria seeks employment. It is not in a typical locale for a bar, but is instead hidden away in the gymnasium of an old high school. When Maria approaches the gym, we first see a close-up of the door leading to it from Maria's point of view. "High school gymnasium" is written in German in black letters on a sign that was perhaps once white and has now turned a faded, yellowish-brown. Then, diagonally running across this sign, the words "off limits" are written in red capital letters. The fact that "off limits" is written in English could have multiple meanings. It could be a warning from the American occupation that all Germans stay away or, more specifically, that white German women should not be fraternizing with Black soldiers. As Timothy Schroer writes:

> Sexual relations between German women and African American soldiers in the [US] army ... represented an acute challenge not only to Nazi racial ideology but also to notions about race more generally shared by Germans and white Americans alike. German officials found it impossible to openly condemn interracial sexual relations per se. They could, however, object to unlawful or immoral conduct that appeared to result from such relations, such as spreading venereal disease, prostitution, and attacks by African Americans on German police officials who tried to enforce laws against German women.[20]

The sign could also be a warning to German men that *they* are not desired here. Such a warning would be unnecessary for white American soldiers, because they preferred not to congregate with Black soldiers and they tended to be the segregating parties rather than the excluded. After the close-up of the sign, we see a reverse shot of Maria pushing the door open and entering the gymnasium. She clearly sees the sign and contemplates what it might mean. But she quickly looks away, as if distracted, and in the next shot, a large American flag hangs to the right of the frame, with half of it out of the frame. The flag is easily recognizable, but it still makes a strange impression as it is hung backwards, with its fifty stars hanging in the upper right-hand corner and only eight of its thirteen stripes visible. The confusing effect of the flag hanging backwards, along with the chaos of old school furniture stacked and stored on the right, perhaps indicates that this is a bizarre space where normative rules don't apply. After all, it is where white German women come to fraternize with African American men out of public view. Her gaze fixed on the flag, Maria is clearly willing to accept whatever problems might come with working in the bar, because fraternizing with American soldiers might just help her make ends meet.

By tackling racism, gender norms, and sexism, *Maria Braun* and the other films in Fassbinder's trilogy provide a critique of West Germany's immediate postwar years, showing German society's transition from the ruins of fascism in the mid-1940s to the glossy, prosperous lifestyles of the 1950s. During an interview about *The Longing of Veronika Voss*, Fassbinder shared his critique of the founding myth of the FRG:

> Our democracy is one that was decreed for the Western zone at the time; we did not fight for it. The old forms have a great ability to look for loopholes, without a swastika of course, but still using the old educational methods. I am amazed how quickly there has been rearmament in this country. . . . I also want to show how the 50s shaped the people of the 60s—this clash between the established and the politically engaged, who were forced into the abnormality of terrorism.[21]

The "old forms" that Fassbinder mentions here are the traditions of authoritarianism and fascism, suggesting Germans may have abandoned Nazism (represented by the swastika) in the postwar period but they have still retained their "old educational methods." Fassbinder was, of course, one among many artists and intellectuals who were concerned with how lingering fascist ideologies affected gender, sex, and race in West Germany.[22] In *Male Fantasies*, published just a year prior to *Maria Braun*'s premiere, Klaus Theweleit explored how German fascist authoritarianism supported misogynistic and racist views. By examining letters, novels and diaries written by white German men both during and after World War I, Theweleit determined that German masculinity was constructed first and foremost as a kind of protection *against* femininity—a fear stemming from the childhood relationship with the mother. In the binary these men created between masculinity and femininity, femininity not only represented irrationality, but was often racialized and associated with the Other, including foreign political groups like the Bolsheviks. By focusing on how masculinity was constructed at this time, Theweleit's work offers a look into the emergence of a notion of German masculinity dependent on whiteness and anxious about purity. Like Fassbinder, Theweleit argues that the demise of the Third Reich did not mean that these views disappeared from society.

Fassbinder's reference to a clash between the establishment and the politically engaged, "who were forced into the abnormality of terrorism," refers to the student revolt of the 1960s. It was during this decade that young West Germans began demanding that the FRG address the persistent authoritarianism that still pervaded society, for instance in that many politicians and judges had served during the Nazi regime and been allowed to remain in or return to power. Things took a drastic turn on June 7, 1967, when student protester Benno Ohnesorg was shot to death by West Berlin police during a demonstration against a state visit to Germany by the Shah of Iran.[23] This moment forced West German students to realize that their democratic state could still find ways to justify legally killing its critics, and from that moment on, many of the protesters became more radicalized, leading to the ultimate radicalization that was the formation of the Red Army Faction. Thus, *Maria Braun* returns to what Fassbinder saw as the source of the FRG's problems, starting with the final years of the Third Reich, which is why the first shot of the film is a black-and-white portrait of Hitler.

An Explosive Beginning

The opening scene of *Maria Braun* is one of the most intriguing in German film history, and it is necessary to unpack this scene, because it establishes the comparison that Fassbinder is ultimately making between Nazi Germany and postwar Germany: both are societies

Figure 1. The opening shot of the film, a portrait of Hitler, with film credits colored red blended in.

that focus on winning at all costs, even if it means sacrificing society's most vulnerable. The portrait of Hitler is the first thing we see (Fig. 1). Hitler is dressed in a suit and tie; he stares straight forward and the camera has captured his right profile. The image appears rather worn and grayish. The diegetic sound we hear is the voice of a pastor, asking Hermann Braun whether he takes Maria to be his lawfully wedded wife. In red cursive, the film's opening credits begin to appear across Hitler's face. The red writing immediately recalls blood. Blood is alluded to because the wedding with which *Maria Braun* opens takes place two years before the end of World War II and in the midst of Allied bombing (Fig. 2).

Maria and Hermann are marrying quickly, during his leave, before he must return to the front. But their marriage appears to be doomed from the start, for immediately after the pastor's words, we hear the sound of a bomb falling. When the registrar tries to flee the building crumbling around them, both Maria and Hermann insist he must stay behind in order to sign their marriage certificate (Fig. 3), which we initially see in an upside-down extreme close-up (Fig. 4), adding

Figure 2. Maria and Hermann can be seen at the altar through the framing of a brick wall damaged by a bomb.

Figure 3. Maria holds onto Hermann, while Hermann restrains the registrar on the ground, forcing him to sign the marriage certificate.

to the disorienting feeling that accompanies the entire opening sequence. Thus, from the very start, this marriage is in a precarious position; between a collapsing building, gunfire, bombing, and the

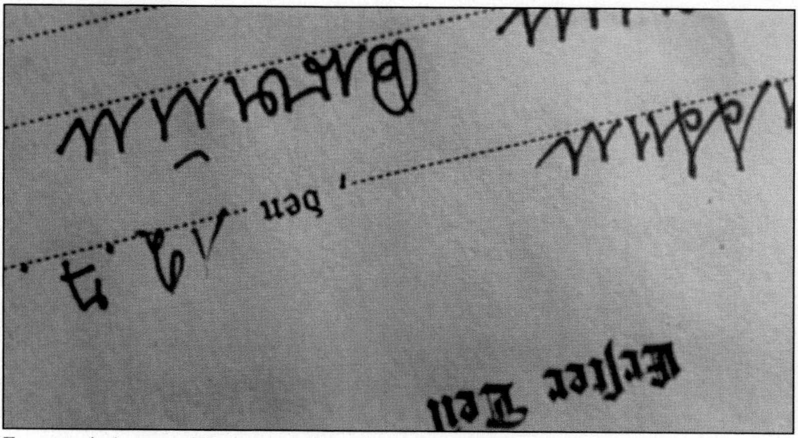

Figure 4. A close-up of Hermann and Maria's marriage certificate.

registrar running off, it just might not happen. And perhaps Maria would have been better off if it hadn't. Her desperate cry of "I can't get out," while she is standing at the window of the civil registry (Fig. 5), serves as a foreshadowing of how her marriage to Hermann and her attempts to navigate her relationships with white men throughout the film will constrict her.

All the elements of the mise-en-scène during the opening sequence—the sounds of bombs dropping, Hitler's image, the blood-red writing—indicate that nothing good lies in store for the Brauns or for Germany. Maria and Hermann's marriage, like Germany's liaison with Hitler, is doomed from the start. But when we encounter Maria in her postwar life, we don't get the sense that Maria has acknowledged the faults of her or her country's past. She is willing to do whatever it takes to survive, but she has still not given up on a past ideal of the perfect life, even if that past ideal has been tainted by the Nazis and their crimes. Maria's unwillingness to truly part with the past is represented by her marriage to Hermann. After the credits, the film cuts to a shot of Maria's mother, standing

Figure 5. Maria and Hermann stand at the window of the civil registry office as other people flee the bombing.

in the kitchen, framed by a hole in the wall created by bombing. A close-up of her hands (Fig. 6) shows her pouring water onto a piece of bread, presumably to soften it now that it's gone stale; an indication of how desperate the times are. Next to a plate of bread, there is a blurry black and white photo of Hermann from the shoulders up, in civilian clothing. Thus, despite his physical absence, the family is still trying to assert his presence in the form of a photograph.

Maria's desire to hold on to the past reflects Alexander and Margarete Mitscherlich's assessment of the postwar German mentality. As they wrote in *The Inability to Mourn* (1975), a psychoanalytic take on West Germany's postwar conscience, "the war was lost; yet though the mountains of rubble it left behind were enormous, there is no denying that Germans did not allow this fact to penetrate their consciousness fully."[24] *Maria Braun* addresses precisely this problem: the problem of Germans who did not or could not properly come to terms with the costs of war and

Figure 6. Maria's mother pours water onto a piece of stale bread.

their own responsibility for the genocide of Jews, Sinti and Roma, Black Germans, gays, socialists, communists, and anyone else whose lives were disregarded by the Nazis. Instead of coming to terms with these crimes, Germans rushed right into the postwar period and, "with the revival of German political influence and economic strength, a fantasy about the past sprang up,"[25] without having really interrogated their beliefs. As Thomas Elsaesser writes, Maria Braun is an allegory for the German nation.[26] She does not give herself time to mourn her marriage and the loss (both mistaken and real) of her husband. She also doesn't take time to come to terms with several difficult, life-changing decisions, such as deciding to "save" Hermann at all costs and possibly choosing to abort her and Bill's baby. Instead, Maria immerses herself in the economic miracle of the 1950s, only to become sorely disappointed with what has become of her life.

Milking Melodrama

One of the unique things about the film's opening scene is the ways in which Fassbinder undermines the genre of the melodrama. Understanding melodrama is important, not just in order to comprehend Fassbinder's unique style but also because of melodrama's usefulness for depicting racialized and gendered conflict on screen. In *Playing the Race Card* (2001), Linda Williams traces the history of race melodrama in an American context, where for centuries melodrama has been "a story cycle brought to life by a circulating set of transmuting icons and melos pointing sometimes to the virtue of racially beset victims and sometimes to the villainy of racially motivated villains."[27]

Prior film scholarship frequently read melodrama as being particularly useful for conveying women's struggles, regardless of their race. According to Thomas Schatz, author of *Hollywood Genres* (1981), in Hollywood "'melodrama' was applied to popular romances that depicted a virtuous individual (usually a woman) or couple (usually lovers) victimized by repressive and inequitable social circumstances, particularly those involving marriage, occupation, and the nuclear family."[28] Thus, like Williams, Schatz emphasizes melodrama's moral struggle between good and evil; in Schatz's case, however, it is only gender that he emphasizes, rather than taking an intersectional approach to this struggle, which is what is necessary for understanding *Maria Braun*. There are at least two ways in which *Maria Braun* undermines the formula Schatz describes. First, rather than a "virtuous woman," Maria is a woman willing to do what it takes to survive and to pursue her idea of happiness, which often involves decisions that would not be described as virtuous in terms of the mores of postwar Germany. For example, her interracial relationship with Bill alone would place her in a space of dishonor. Secondly, a typical thematic of the melodrama is "the ambiguous function of marriage (as simultaneously sexually liberating and socially restricting)."²⁹ A melodrama typically *ends* with a marriage. *The Marriage of Maria Braun*, by contrast, begins with one. Thus, due to Fassbinder's inversion of this trope, viewers may suspect that there will be no happy ending at the conclusion of this narrative. Instead, by the conclusion of the film, we've witnessed a couple who never spent more than a day together in married bliss.

It is partly because of how Fassbinder combines melodrama with techniques of arthouse cinema that *Maria Braun* has been dubbed Fassbinder's "German Hollywood film" and became his most popular film. Not only did the film turn him into the best-paid director in Germany, but even overseas, in the United States, the film earned over a million dollars during its first year in theaters.³⁰ In order for *Maria Braun* to appeal to this larger market at home and abroad, Fassbinder had to make a compromise by combining the estranging aesthetics he had become known for with a more conventional, straightforward narrative. One of the aesthetic practices in *Maria Braun* that he continued from previous films is a heavy reliance on intertexts and citations.

Citationality is a key element of melodramatic films about race, because these films mobilize racist stereotypes that must be performed again and again in order to maintain their believability. As Homi Bhabha writes, racial stereotyping is "knowledge and identification that vacillates between what is always already known, and something that's repeated as if the essential duplicity of the Asiatic or the bestial sexual license of the African that needs no proof, can never really, in discourse, be proved."³¹ Melodramas both participate in generating stereotypical images about Black people *and* rely on past racist images that have been circulated in film.³²

In early American cinema, melodramas participated in this racist discourse by juxtaposing the virtue of "innocent" white characters against the "immoral behavior" of Black characters. Linda Williams describes this as a negrophilic/negrophobic cycle, because while these narratives perpetuated fear of Black people (negrophobia), early American race films also conveyed a degree of (forbidden) desire for Blackness (negrophilia); a desire that had to be expressed in socially acceptable ways, such as through blackface.[33] By wearing blackface in these melodramas, white Americans could both enjoy masquerading as and viewing the Other, while villainizing and ridiculing them simultaneously. According to Williams, it is this need to reproduce these Black stereotypes that requires a degree of citationality in each film: "each new incarnation of this negrophilic/ negrophobic cycle cites a previous version of the Tom or anti-Tom story of racial victims and villains, sometimes reversing the moral polarities, sometimes simply appropriating old polarities in new ways."[34] William's reference to the Tom and anti-Tom draws on white American abolitionist Harriet Beecher Stowe's novel *Uncle Tom's Cabin* (1852). Although Stowe intended the book to make an argument *against* slavery by depicting the dehumanizing conditions enslaved Blacks were subjected to, the book's legacy has also been that of creating an equally dehumanizing caricature of Black subservience. Uncle Tom is an elderly enslaved man on the plantation who, despite years of abuse, appeals to the other enslaved Blacks to approach their white masters with grace and forgiveness, rather than vengeance. But it was through the medium of film that the sympathy *Uncle Tom's Cabin* generated among white Americans towards the plight of enslaved Blacks would be shifted towards Southern whites. It was D. W. Griffith's racist film about the founding of the Ku Klux Klan, *The Birth of a Nation* (1915), that convinced many white Americans that the once-disparaged Southern understanding of the Civil War and Reconstruction was actually historical truth. It was so popular that then-President Woodrow Wilson held a special screening for it at the White House on February 18, 1915; it was the *first* film ever screened at the White House. Griffith generated hatred for Black people by introducing white Americans to the "anti-Tom," a figure who fed on white Americans fears since slavery was abolished that newly liberated Blacks would seek revenge. White men believed that slavery was useful for protecting white womanhood against allegedly hypersexual Black men who lusted after white women. The "anti-Tom" became the symbol of the feared, Black male rapist. This, according to Williams, is how *Birth of a Nation* converted sympathy for Blacks who conformed to the Uncle Tom stereotype to an antipathy against those seen as "anti-Toms" and as sexual threats to white women.[35] While Fassbinder does not directly cite Griffith, he is still mobilizing the same stereotypes as Griffith: by introducing characters like Bill and Lonely Richard, he plays on white Germans' fears of Black men "violating" white German women. Thus, by using melodrama in *Maria Braun* to portray gendered and racial conflict, Fassbinder is ultimately relying on the racial stereotypes portrayed in previous films that have done the same, both in American films *and* German films, like Paul Verhoeven's *Gottes zweite Garnitur* (1967), about a white German woman who has an affair with a Black GI.

Drama in Black and White

Because Douglas Sirk's work was so influential in Fassbinder's approach to staging racial and gendered conflicts through melodrama, it is useful to consider what exactly Fassbinder borrowed from Sirk. John Mercer and Martin Shingler describe *Maria Braun* as one of the films in which Fassbinder uses "stylistic devices borrowed from Sirk," namely the "Sirkian use of vivid colour."[36] But Sirk's influence on Fassbinder's films actually began much earlier, starting somewhere between the filming of *Pioneers in Ingolstadt* (1971) and *The Merchant of Four Seasons* (1972). Fassbinder became interested in Sirk's work in 1971, when he saw a retrospective of Sirk's films at the Film Museum in Munich. Afterwards, Fassbinder tracked Sirk down, visiting him in Ascona, Switzerland.[37]

Fassbinder hoped to learn from Sirk's ability to explore the emotional realm of a person's private life, while always acknowledging how the personal and political interact. Fassbinder argued that both his and Sirk's films were interested in people trying to survive in a society that was hostile towards them, which at the time was arguably the case for any character who was not a straight white man. Anton Kaes points out that a lot of the techniques Fassbinder borrowed from Sirk—"making filmic space itself signify through high-contrast lighting, [and] through the symbolic use of everyday objects"—came from Sirk's early work as a theater director.[38] The directors also shared thematic interests. Like Fassbinder, in his day Sirk was daring enough to tackle issues of race, gender, and class. Of Sirk's films, the one that was most centered on race was *Imitation of Life*.

In true melodramatic fashion, in *Imitation of Life* Sirk places his white protagonist at the center of several moral quandaries: 1) she can become a star, but she may have to let herself be sexually exploited in exchange for a role; 2) she can pursue acting *or* marry her long-term lover, Steve; 3) she can become a successful actress *or* be a good mother like Annie. Ultimately, she tries to pursue acting without compromising her ideals, but she can never make everyone happy at once. And, as for Annie, even though she is the picture-perfect mother, her daughter Sarah Jane loathes her for "cursing" her with her African American heritage and her insistence on interfering any time Sarah Jane tries to pass as white. All that Annie desires for herself is a decadent funeral, so that everyone who respects and admires her will show up to the occasion. Fassbinder remarks about this scene: "None of the protagonists come to see that everything, thoughts, desires, dreams arise directly from social reality or are manipulated by it."[39] This last statement could just as easily be said about Maria Braun.

In *Maria Braun*, Fassbinder adopts many of the themes and techniques he learned from Sirk. There are several scenes where interplays of color and light in the form of lighting, makeup, and vibrant clothing allow Maria to stand out against her drab surroundings. In a scene where Betti is doing Maria's hair (see Fig. 7),

Figure 7. Betti does Maria's hair in front of a mirror.

we see close-up of Maria wearing a thick layer of white makeup, almost resembling a pantomime. The exaggerated nature of her makeup in this scene draws attention both to the constructed nature of gender and to Maria's performative nature. The white foundation combined with her bright red lipstick contrast even more with the dark background thanks to the frontal lighting that illuminates Maria, while casting Betti in the shadows. This lighting may serve as a metaphor for Maria's later success thanks to her ability to seize opportunities. Maria will climb the ladder of success, while Betti remains the dowdy housewife with whom her husband grows tired.

This scene also demonstrates how, in addition to using color and lighting, sound and framing are also key to Fassbinder's depiction of the conflicts that arise around interracial romance and social mobility. This scene begins with Betti and Maria singing "Nur nicht aus Liebe weinen," a song whose significance I will discuss below. Most importantly, it is an example of how Fassbinder uses popular music pointedly to comment on his characters. As Betti removes the curlers from Maria's hair, they fall to her vanity making clinking sounds, almost like bullets falling. Once Maria's hair is finished, she remarks that her hairstyle looks like a poodle, but she doesn't mind because "Americans are crazy for poodles." Her remark is immediately followed by a close-up of a black and white picture of Hermann in uniform (see Fig. 8), which is covered by piles of curlers and makeup.

Just as in previous scenes, these close-ups of Hermann's photos throughout the household make it known that despite his physical absence, he is always present in Maria's mind. But the fact that she would allow his photo to be buried under these curlers indicates that her mind might be becoming more occupied with finding another suitor—specifically an American suitor who is into "poodles." Betti's look of shock—which is exaggerated by the same stark, white foundation Maria is wearing—conveys to us what German society thinks of Maria if she is truly considering starting a relationship with an American soldier. In terms of race, one could also interpret their white makeup as Fassbinder's attempt to show us how much whiteness is valued in this society, which is why Maria's ultimate choice of Bill will be such a transgression. Sleeping with Bill is one of several transgressive steps Maria Braun will make in her pursuit of financial security. And just as Sirk's protagonist Lora fails in her own pursuits, because she cannot be both a "decent" mother and wife and a star, in Fassbinder's film, Maria must also fail, because the system is rigged against anyone who isn't a straight white male.

Love Stories Set in a War Zone

On the one hand, Sirk's films were progressive, because they focused on marginalized people—for instance women, and specifically older women and Black women. On the other hand, Sirk did not necessarily question or undermine the morality at work in the melodrama. For a melodrama to function, there have to be morally good and morally bad characters. In Sirk's *Imitation of Life*, for example, Annie is the

Figure 8. A close-up of a worn picture of Hermann lying beneath piles of curlers and makeup.

morally good character, akin to the "magical Negro," defined by Cerise L. Glenn as "wise, morally upright Blacks who served as the moral conscience of White characters."[40] As the "magical Negro," Annie exists to support and improve white characters' lives. She does not question her station in life. When Sarah Jane curses her for ruining her own attempts at passing, Annie learns to reconcile herself to her daughter's feelings, and she is rewarded with an elaborate funeral at which half the town is present, even the daughter who once rejected her. But the reality is that social conflicts around race, gender, and class can rarely be explained in such a cut-and-dried manner. In reality, it would be difficult to imagine that a mother like Annie would be happy sacrificing herself for her daughter, even willing to keep her identity a secret for her daughter's sake, and asking for nothing in return. The truth is, there is always a morally gray area when it comes to the sacrifices a mother is willing to make for her child. This is perhaps better conveyed in a melodrama like *Stella Dallas* (1937), where the sacrificial mother is largely concerned with her own self-image even when she does something for the sake of her child. Thus, trying to portray any character as purely morally good, without flaws, is unrealistic. And though Annie may have been an easy character to cast as morally good due to her status as a "simple" Black maid, it would be much harder to cast Germans living under the Nazi regime in such a role, which is precisely what Sirk attempted to do in *A Time to Love and a Time to Die* (1958).

A Time to Love and a Time to Die is based on a novel by the German author Erich Maria Remarque, who plays a small role in the film as the antifascist Professor Pohlmann. In this film, one can clearly see how Sirk's commitment to melodrama causes him to shortchange some of the ambiguity of wartime Germany that Fassbinder, even just in the very opening sequence of *Maria Braun*, emphasizes.[41] *A Time to Love and a Time to Die* shows us some of the historical context that we don't see in *Maria Braun*, namely what life is like for disillusioned German soldiers on the Eastern front in 1944, a year before the end of the war. The protagonist of the film is Ernst Graeber. He has not been home for two years. During his leave, he happens to meet Elizabeth, the adult daughter of a family acquaintance. In true melodramatic form, despite a frosty beginning, Ernst wins the reluctant Elizabeth over, and their brief first date, which ends prematurely due to an air raid, is quickly followed by a marriage proposal.

Because *Maria Braun* begins with Maria and Hermann's marriage, we don't see their courtship. We must simply accept Maria's words at face value: that she truly loves Hermann so much that she couldn't possibly love another man the same way. In contrast, in Sirk's film we know that Elizabeth and Ernst have only known each other for a few days. But due to the conventions of melodrama, we must accept that despite the briefness of the time they've had together, they have fallen madly in love with each other, and that this is the true reason why Elizabeth agrees to marry Ernst—not just for the money she would be entitled to as the wife of a soldier. The remainder of the film includes a number of twists and turns to heighten the dramatic action. On the couple's final night together, before Ernst must return to the front, the pair is hopeful. Elizabeth has found shelter in a nice home that has been untouched by the bombing. She hopes that she and Ernst will one day have a house full of children—a desire that Maria Braun never expresses. In fact, we know of only one pregnancy in Maria's life—the child she conceives with Bill.[42] And it's implied that she decides to terminate that pregnancy after she kills Bill. Perhaps she does so because raising a child alone while Hermann is in jail would only make it more difficult for her to get back on her feet. Perhaps she is not prepared to live with the stigma of raising a biracial child, a postwar dilemma I will elaborate on below. In any case, part of what makes Maria Braun an antihero is that she does not aspire to the conventions that are supposed to make a woman happy.

In the final scenes of *A Time to Love*, Ernst is back at the front, where he receives a letter from Elizabeth announcing that she is pregnant. Ernst is not only joyful, but resolute that he is no longer willing to participate in the Nazis' genocide. When a fellow soldier informs him that he must shoot several civilian prisoners, Ernst not only refuses, but shoots his compatriot instead, before freeing the prisoners. However, his moral resolve will be the end of him. One of the prisoners takes the gun from Ernst's compatriot and shoots Ernst before escaping. In the film's final shot, Ernst has collapsed over the railing of a bridge. His face is reflected in the water below him as he desperately tries to hold onto hope in the form of Elizabeth's letter. But the letter floats beyond his grasp and he dies.

We know that Fassbinder saw *A Time to Love and a Time to Die*, as he includes an analysis of it in his essay, "Six Films by Douglas Sirk."[43] But though Sirk's war film may share some themes with *Maria Braun*, Fassbinder chooses to focus on the experience of the woman left waiting at home rather than to show the war through the soldier's eyes.[44] Furthermore, instead of attempting to convey an authentic love, the film never gives Maria and Hermann's love story much screen time after their tumultuous wedding day. Even when Hermann returns from the front, their love story keeps getting delayed: by Maria's killing of Bill, by Hermann's serving time in prison instead of her, and finally by Oswald's deal with Hermann for him to stay away. While Sirk's film largely follows convention, focusing on the innocent Elizabeth and Ernst, the jaded soldier who refuses to do wrong, Fassbinder's heroine is far from innocent, precisely because she will need her wits to help her stay alive, both in the immediate aftermath of the war and during the rebuilding of the 1950s. As one cynical American reviewer wrote at the time of the film's release: "almost everybody will be a sucker for Maria Braun. So what if she is without remorse for the Nazis' deeds? So what if she marries a Nazi soldier? She experiences enough agony in her life (because her man is in jail, she has love affairs but not love) that we forgive her transgressions."[45]

Undermining Melodrama

When watching *A Time to Love*, one notices, in addition to the subject matter, a lot of stylistic characteristics that Fassbinder borrowed from Sirk. Kaes describes them as "'unrealistic' lighting, obtrusive camera movements, and artificial highly stylized décor."[46] Obtrusive camera movements are used when Ernst first returns home from the front for his leave. The camera's placement behind debris obscures him as he walks among the rubble searching for his home. In this scene, Sirk also uses sound to deceive his viewers. As Ernst searches for his parents' apartment building among the rubble, an eerie sound in a minor chord seems to be non-diegetic, indicating that his parents have met a tragic end. But we soon discover, along with Ernst, that the eerie noise is coming from the wind blowing against the string of a piano that's been destroyed in the bombing. This play with sound together with the obtrusive camera movements set viewers on an emotional roller coaster, keeping us in suspense as to whether or not Ernst will find his family. One example of Sirk's unrealistic lighting is in a scene between Ernst and Elizabeth when they first meet and are standing in her room. Despite Elizabeth's room being relatively well lit, the mirror is uncannily dark, to the point that it doesn't even show Ernst's reflection when he stands before it. This perhaps conveys Elizabeth's initial distrust of Ernst; as the daughter of a concentration camp prisoner, she cannot be sure of Ernst's political beliefs. Finally, the gaudy gold decorations of the illegal restaurant where Ernst takes Elizabeth for their first date are an example of "artificial highly stylized décor." While the rest of the city is consistently shown in gray and drab tones, due to its state of disarray from the war, the colorful, shiny flourishes of the restaurant create an atmosphere of fantasy, where Ernst and Elizabeth can briefly escape their troubles and fall in love.

Despite borrowing from Sirk's style, Fassbinder also actively sought to *undermine* melodramatic conventions. In an interview, Fassbinder once stated that although he and Sirk shared similar aesthetics (such as framing and the use of mirrors and bright colors) and subject matter, Sirk could not risk being as openly critical of society due to his having to work within the Hollywood system. Fassbinder describes Sirk's critiques as "soft, subliminal." As a result of working from within Hollywood, Sirk's films tend to convey a black-and-white view of the morality of his characters, while Fassbinder's films convey a complex and ambiguous view of his characters. This is evident when one compares *Maria Braun* to *A Time to Love and a Time to Die*: the latter does not explore any of the moral gray areas of the war. Despite the fact that the main characters are Germans (a Nazi soldier and his new bride), Sirk frames both characters as innocent victims caught up in the difficult circumstances of the war and oppressed by the Gestapo and military officers. Unlike Fassbinder, Sirk doesn't consider the complicity in the Nazi regime of those Germans who were innocent of war crimes. While it is commonplace in melodramas to portray characters being "at the mercy of social conventions,"[47] Fassbinder shows us that Maria is very much actively involved in her own oppression. She has numerous opportunities to free herself from her bond to Hermann, such as through her relationship with Bill, but she chooses not to, because, first, she doesn't believe that she has a choice and, second, she thinks she can exist within the system of patriarchy and oppression while still gaining the upper hand. She believes that by influencing Hermann and Oswald, she can flee the "strictures of social and familial tradition" without having to leave these men behind.[48]

Part of how Fassbinder undermines melodrama is by depicting the reconciliation of soldiers and their war brides as disappointing rather than fulfilling desire. Fassbinder gives his protagonist something she has yearned for, something she *believes* she desires—namely Hermann's return—but in giving her what she desires, Fassbinder reveals that, first, we don't always know what we really want and, second, when we do get what we want, we're not necessarily happy with it. Lauren Berlant has made a similar argument about the "cruel optimism" of life under neoliberalism: we grow attached to possibilities that are "discovered either to be *im*possible, sheer fantasy, or *too* possible, and toxic."[49]

Fassbinder's Style

Despite Fassbinder's manipulation of melodramatic conventions, which made the film so popular with audiences, there are nevertheless particular characteristics that keep *Maria Braun* very much in line with the rest of Fassbinder's oeuvre and continue the theme of portraying the oppression of people existing on the margins. Even with Fassbinder's attempts throughout his life to distance himself from Bertolt Brecht, the mood that Fassbinder creates in *Maria Braun* is, at times, comparable to Brecht's alienation effect.[50] Take, for example, Fassbinder's preference for anti-naturalist acting, something that became a point of contention between Fassbinder and the lead actress, Hanna Schygulla, prior to filming *Maria Braun*. The film scholar Johannes von Moltke describes Schygulla's performance in the film as often being like that of a drag performer: "she is not simply a woman of the fifties, but one [a woman] who is constantly playing a woman of the fifties."[51] As a result of these alienating aesthetics, one American reviewer even asked: "is he [Fassbinder] afraid that without this intellectual distance, we'd admire her?"[52] And perhaps this reviewer is right about that, because we *aren't* supposed to admire Maria. From an uncritical perspective, Maria may appear to be the kind of heroine one should root for. She finds a way, despite all odds, to survive, even thrive. But she does so to the detriment of others who are structurally in less advantageous positions than she is, like the Black men she uses. She betrays the working class when she is working for Oswald and negotiates a contract to their detriment; and she disregards the feelings of the other women in her life, like her mother and Betti. Thus, Fassbinder's inclusion of alienating aesthetics in the film may have less to do with his needing to put his particular touch on it and more to do with him not wanting us to simply root for or condemn Maria. While Hollywood melodramas like *Imitation of Life* and *Stella Dallas* encouraged audiences to denounce female characters for their "immorality," Fassbinder wants his audience to think critically about Maria and interrogate the circumstances that influence her actions.

This feeling of artificiality is even conveyed through the smallest of props, such as when Maria brings home a pack of cigarettes that she was given by an American soldier at the train station and offers one to her mother. Prior to the stabilization of the German market in 1949, cigarettes functioned as a form of currency on the black market. Fassbinder wants us to remember how much of a fetish object cigarettes were during this era, due to Germans' desperate economic circumstances. To accomplish that, he follows the brief conversation between Maria and her mother with an extreme close-up of two packs of Camel cigarettes (Fig. 9).

Figure 9. An extreme close-up of packs of Camel cigarettes in Maria' kitchen.

Another part of this artificiality and a key element of Fassbinder's auteur style was that he would play small cameos in his own films. In *Maria Braun*, he is a black-market dealer (Fig. 10) to whom Maria gives her mother's brooch, exchanging it for a tight black V-neck dress that she then wears to secure the bar job and a bottle of alcohol for her mother to drink, to drown her worries about her daughter's moral well-being. After selling Maria these items, which she views as helping to secure her economic security and a brief moment of distraction, Fassbinder's character then tries to sell her a 1907 edition of the complete works of Heinrich von Kleist. This reference to Kleist is something that Fassbinder added to the shooting script.[53] Kleist was one of many Romantic German authors whom the Nazis tried to enmesh within their cultural politics, demonstrated by Leni Riefenstahl's never-completed film adaptation of *Penthesilea*[54] and Emil Jannings's award-winning performance in a film adaptation of *The Broken Jug* (1937), which the Nazis interpreted as "a lighthearted accolade to authoritarianism and order."[55] Thus, when Maria rejects the deal's offer by responding, "Books burn so easily and they don't keep you warm," she can both be rejecting the Nazis and suggesting

Figure 10. Fassbinder makes a cameo in the film as a black-market dealer.

that literature no longer has value because it cannot distract Germans from their current hardships and, in any case, it was unable to protect Germany from fascism. Thus, this brief, humorous cameo allows Fassbinder to yet again connect the values of the postwar period to those of the Nazi period (by alluding to book burnings) and to inform the audience of what *really* has value in this postwar period, namely sex and alcohol, while classic German literature has become valueless.

Another important alienation effect that Fassbinder employs is sound. As in most of his films, the music for this film was composed by Peer Raben, whom Fassbinder had known since his early days working in the Anti-Theater in Munich.[56] In addition to the diegetic and non-diegetic music, throughout the film there are different, competing sounds layered on top of each other. During the opening sequence of the film, for example, in addition to the sounds of gunfire and bombs, and sentimental instrumental music in a minor chord, a baby's cry can be heard offscreen. This crying serves as a metaphor— the next generation of Germans are crying as they are born into a world of destruction left to them by their parents. This anticipates

Helma Sanders-Brahms's use of the metaphor of childbirth in *Germany, Pale Mother* (1980), where the main protagonist, Lene, gives birth to a daughter during an air raid. Images of Lene naked and screaming in childbirth are intercut with color footage of bombed-out German cities from a bird's-eye view. In *Maria Braun*, meanwhile, the baby's cry, in addition to serving as a commentary on the legacy of war for Germany's intergenerational conflict, also foreshadows Maria's possible decision to abort her baby after she kills Bill. Aborting the baby would save Maria from two potential challenges. First, she would be able to work without having to find childcare, the problem faced by the protagonists of *Imitation of Life*. And furthermore, she wouldn't have to face the moral judgment and condemnation of a public that did not treat the white mothers of Black German children kindly. Thus, the baby's crying at the start of the film foreshadows the suffering of the postwar generation as well as Maria's choice of self-preservation over motherhood.

Another use of sound unique to Fassbinder is the emphasis on what one would otherwise typically hear as background noise. In *Maria Braun*, such sounds are frequently called attention to, allowing them to drown out the dialogue between the characters. This is a technique that Fassbinder subsequently used in films like *The Third Generation* (1979) and *The Longing of Veronika Voss* (1981). In fact, the most significant audio at the end of *Maria Braun*—that of a radio broadcast of the 1954 World Cup final between Germany and Hungary taking place in Bern, with play-by-play from Herbert Zimmermann—can also be heard in *Lola*, another film in the BRD trilogy.[57] As Joyce Rheuban has noted, using this broadcast to connect the two films is a nod to "both the chronological overlapping of the films and the socio-historical continuity which links their narratives."[58] In *Maria Braun*, the broadcast begins towards the end of the film, while Maria is dining alone at the Bastion restaurant following the death of her employer and lover Oswald. When Maria stands up to leave, she suddenly feels faint and has to grab onto a column to steady herself. Several male waiters rush to her aid, and as the camera pulls back, we see that while Maria is struggling to regain composure in the background behind closed glass doors at the center of the frame, in the foreground to the left of the frame, in a separate room, two members of the staff, a man and a woman, are passionately kissing. The man stands behind the woman and she has her back turned toward him, facing the camera. As he kisses the left side of her neck, he simultaneously fondles her naked breasts, which are in plain view for the audience, exposed because the top half of her uniform has been unbuttoned. Here, Fassbinder emphasizes a clash between vulgarity and decorum, life and death. Maria's relationship with Oswald has ended due to his death, while these young people's passionate behavior represents life. While Maria is sitting at her table, the radio plays a speech by Adenauer about Germany's decision to rearm, but as soon as the intimate pair is revealed, the radio switches to a broadcast of the 1954 World Cup game. Fassbinder suggests that West Germany might have seemed decent and respectable on the surface, but beneath the polite rhetoric, such as Adenauer's earlier denial of any intent to rearm, there is actually a layer of vulgarity—nationalism, greed, and authoritarianism. Finally, Fassbinder also intimates that while West Germans might think of politicians like Adenauer as what unites them, the glue that holds West Germans together is actually something as common as soccer through national identification with a team and the desire to be victors again.

The World Cup broadcast is not the only instance of radio being utilized as background noise in the film. In the family apartment, at the start of the film, when Maria returns from the black market, we hear a radio announcer state that he is interrupting a performance of Beethoven's Ninth Symphony in order to read a list of the names of soldiers who are still missing. The announcer states that there is a message waiting for each name he calls. We never actually get to hear Beethoven's Ninth, just the interruption and then the list of names, which the announcer proceeds to read as Maria and her mother continue talking. Like Fassbinder's witty comments during his cameo, this interruption indicates that German high culture has been disturbed by the brutalities of war. Maria and her mother presumably keep the broadcast on because they have also left a message for Hermann and they are hoping that he is listening to the same broadcast. The possibility that Maria and Hermann could be listening to the same broadcast, even while physically being apart, helps her maintain the fantasy that the bond between them is still strong. The diegetic sound of the names bleeds into the next scene, when we see Maria at a train station searching for Hermann, wearing a sandwich-board sign bearing his name and other identifying information about him.

Fassbinder uses the radio to offer historical context in several subsequent scenes, such as when Maria's announcement to her family that she is moving out and will be working for Oswald is accompanied by a radio report about West German rearmament. According to Wolfgang Gast, this text, rather than quoting one specific speech, is a montage of different speeches by Adenauer that Fassbinder strung together.[59] In this scene, Adenauer's insistence that Germany isn't interested in building a new army is juxtaposed with a subsequent radio report, from several years later, in which we hear Adenauer insist on Germany's right to rearmament, revealing a certain degree of hypocrisy and the ability of West Germans to quickly forget the lessons of the past.

Music

Music plays a central role in *Maria Braun*. It allows Fassbinder both to achieve a balance between melodrama and arthouse film and to introduce further intertexts that emphasize the continuity between fascist and post-fascist Germany and Maria Braun's role as the ultimate embodiment of the willingness to sacrifice real social change for the superficial social change implied by economic success.

Throughout *Maria Braun*, Fassbinder incorporates historical music to serve as a commentary not only on the 1940s, but on his present. In an early scene, when Maria laments that there are no men to come home to anymore, she is happily surprised to find Grandpa Berger in the apartment she shares with her mother. Rather than being biologically related to Maria, Grandpa Berger is her mother's boyfriend. Based on Maria's conversations with her mother, it appears their relationship is based on convenience and survival. Later on, when the money Maria provides allows her mother to wear nicer clothes and find a younger boyfriend, her mother quips that Grandpa Berger "at least kept her warm in those cold times after the war," a remark that both references his stockpile of firewood and their previous romantic relationship.

When we first see Grandpa Berger, prior to Maria's arrival, he is sitting in the kitchen, quietly humming the "Horst-Wessel-Lied" (The Horst Wessel Song) to himself, as we hear an announcer on the radio list the names of missing people (Fig. 11). The "Horst-Wessel-Lied" was introduced by the Nazis as a second German national

Figure 11. Grandpa Berger sits in the kitchen humming to himself.

anthem in 1933. The lyrics were written by Horst Wessel (1907–1930), a member of the *Sturmabteilung* (SA) and set to a traditional tune. Because he was murdered during the *Kampfzeit*—a period during which the Nazis and communists vied for political influence through open battles in the streets—Wessel was considered a Nazi martyr after his death. Grandpa Berger's humming of this song indicates that he, and his generation along with him, is still caught in the past, neither mentally nor physically ready to move on from the Nazi period. Maria's mother silences him, saying "Shame on you," an indication of the collective shame felt by Germans, as explored in Alexander and Margarete Mitscherlich's book *The Inability to Mourn*, mentioned above.

Another moment when music is used as a marker of the past is when a man at the black market can be overheard lamenting that one can no longer play the "Deutschlandlied" (Song of Germany). The lyrics for the "Deutschlandlied" were taken from a poem written by Heinrich von Fallersleben in 1841 that protested against the tyranny and censorship of the German nobility. Von Fallersleben belonged to the nineteenth-century German democratic movement. Much of the impetus for the movement was that there was no unified German state at the time, much less a democratic one. In his poem, von Fallersleben describes what he views as the geographic borders of a potential German democratic nation, naming several waterways currently found in Italy, Belgium, Denmark, and Lithuania: "From the Meuse to the Neman, / From the Adige to the Belt." The "Deutschlandlied" was used as the country's official national anthem starting in 1922. The Nazis then adopted von Fallersleben's lyrics as a rebuke against the Versailles Treaty, which had taken away several of Germany's territories following World War I. The Nazis viewed von Fallersleben's lyrics as reflecting their desire to unite German-speaking peoples and lands under one government. In the postwar period, the song had strong and problematic nationalist overtones due to the Nazis' use of it. Since the end of the World War II, whenever the German national anthem is sung in the FRG, only the third stanza—about unity, justice, and freedom—is sung.

Even when Fassbinder employs popular music in *Maria Braun*, it serves as a marker for how the past shows up in the present. Take, for example, Zarah Leander's song "Nur nicht aus Liebe weinen" (Just Don't Cry for Love), which Maria and her friend Betti sing while they are applying makeup in front of the mirror before going out for the night (Fig. 12). This song was not originally present in the shooting script; it was added by Fassbinder.[60] Leander (1907–1981), the Swedish star who was the leading female star of Nazi Germany, appeared in several Nazi film productions. She performs this particular song in Carl Fröhlich's film *It Was a Gay Ball Night*. Fassbinder's reference to this film demonstrates his familiarity with German film history, and his integration of a wartime film icon into *Maria Braun* demonstrates the continuity between the war and the postwar period, in this case indicting Maria's actions in the film by comparing her with Leander. In order to better understand why such a comparison is detrimental, it is important to consider

Figure 12. Betti and Maria applying makeup and singing.

Leander's legacy of starring in films produced by the Nazis. After the staunch antifascist Marlene Dietrich opted to remain in America after following the director Josef von Sternberg there in 1930, Leander became the darling of the Nazi film industry. Leander was recruited to work in Nazi film while she was in Vienna, working as an operetta and revue singer. She was deemed a good fit for Nazi cinema because she had shown a talent for mimicking icons, such as when she took on Dietrich's role in a Swedish remake of *Der Blaue Engel* (The Blue Angel, 1930).[61] Working for the Nazis, she frequently starred in revues, musical melodramas, and musical films like *It Was a Gay Ball Night*.

Fröhlich's film contains several themes that resonate with *Maria Braun*, all connected with how the oppressive nature of gender roles can negatively impact heterosexual relationships. *It Was a Gay Ball Night* concerns a love triangle between the Russian composer Tchaikovsky, his former lover, Katja, played by Leander, and Katja's husband, Mikhail Murakin. As the title of the film suggests, Katja and Tchaikovsky encounter each other at a masked ball featuring his compositions. Tchaikovsky laments that he is unable to focus on his music because he is seeking patronage and therefore doesn't have time to focus on his music. He also expresses the desire to rekindle their affair, even though he is engaged to the dancer Nastasja Petrovna. Katja rejects his romantic advances, but because of her love for him, she decides to anonymously fund his work. When they meet again at a subsequent performance, Tchaikovsky is over the moon about how productive he has been thanks to the money he has received. But he would still like to rekindle their romance. This puts Katja in a difficult position. She is paying for Tchaikovsky's music with her husband's money. So she can't leave her husband to be with Tchaikovsky, because then she could no longer secretly fund his work, which would have a negative effect on his productivity. There are similarities here to the situation in which Maria Braun finds herself in her relationship with Oswald. Maria believes that maintaining a romantic relationship with Oswald will help her set aside enough wealth to fund a life for Hermann and her together, once Hermann is released from prison. But Oswald and Hermann take this choice away from her, secretly coming to their own agreement about when Hermann and Maria should be reunited—an arrangement that Hermann only agrees to because it allows him access to his own money, provided by Oswald, which he needs in order to maintain his sense of masculinity and feel like he is in control of Maria, rather than the other way around. Even though Oswald is giving Hermann the money in exchange for him staying away from Maria, in Hermann's eyes that is better than having to accept "Maria's" money, that is, the money *she* has gotten from Oswald.

In Fröhlich's film, Katja decides that she can't see Tchaikovsky again, because if he knew it was her money funding his work, he'd lose his pride; thus, the film points out the connections between masculinity, pride, and money that Fassbinder also makes central to *Maria Braun*. On the day of Tchaikovsky's marriage to Nastasja, Katja's husband throws a party (separate from Tchaikovsky's nuptial celebrations) and his guests ask Katja to sing something. She sings "Just Don't Cry for Love," whose lyrics introduce a motif that will be repeated throughout the film. In singing that there is not only one man to love, because there are so many men in this world, Katja is trying to convince herself not to mourn her relationship with Tchaikovsky. She has to sacrifice romantic love for both her own and Tchaikovsky's economic stability. And thus, when Maria and Betti sing this same song in Fassbinder's film, the song foreshadows Maria's ultimate dilemma: you can't have money *and* the love of your life.

Because of the reference to Leander (who became a gay icon to filmmakers of Fassbinder's generation)[62] when Betti and Maria sing to each other, and because of the heavy makeup they both wear in this scene, Ulrike Sieglohr claims that this performance of Leander's song not only works as a "camp reference for some gay people" but also "simultaneously put[s] an image of two attractive women (Schygulla and Trissenaar) on display for the heterosexual gaze."[63] Furthermore, Erica Carter points out that "musically, 'Nur nicht aus Liebe weinen,' for instance may well evoke the polymorphous sexualities, the exotic ethnic affiliations and gender transgressions of Weimar, but the lyrics remind Leander's listeners of the imperative that such desires end in renunciation."[64] It is through songs like this that Fassbinder sets the stage for postwar German history, using visual and audio cues to transport viewers back in time. But these cues are not necessarily intended for those Germans who actually lived through this period; instead, they are for those of a younger generation who grew up hearing *about* it.

A War Widow?

After the credits roll, the film immediately transitions to the war's aftermath. Though the war has ended, Hermann has not yet returned. In Germany, by the end of the war, at least four million men were dead. According to the 1946 census, 56 percent of the population was female, and by 1949, only 43 percent of West German women were married.[65] This is why the symbol of Germany's rebuilding at this time was the *Trümmerfrau* (rubble woman), the women who cleared the rubble after the war (Fig. 13).

Given the shortage of men, German women had to step up and take on a more significant role outside of the household as providers and protectors. It is implied that Maria's father, Karl, died in the war and now her mother secretly trades his old clothes for some firewood from Grandpa Berger. She doesn't want Maria to know, in case it might hurt her pride. But Maria is not sentimental about her father's things. She says matter-of-factly: "Father is dead and we're alive." This sober attitude is exactly what will help Maria not only survive but thrive during the postwar period. It is this lack of sentimentality that allows her to quickly choose Hermann

Figure 13. A *Trümmerfrau*, West Germany, 1950. Bundesarchiv, Bild 183-S94177. Photo by Rudolf, March 7, 1950.

over Bill, despite how close she and Bill had grown in Hermann's absence. Like many of Fassbinder's heroines, especially those in the BRD trilogy, Maria is a strong woman and a survivor. Though Germany has crumbled to pieces around her, she does what it takes to keep going. That she must do so causes resentment on her part towards German men, a resentment that is revealed in several different scenes. But her mother also takes a practical approach to her relationships with men. When her husband Karl dies, she enters a relationship with Grandpa Berger in order to "keep warm."

And years later, when the family is financially better off, she trades in Grandpa Berger for a new, younger lover. When her mother remarks that Grandpa Berger kept her warm during the war, her new boyfriend thinks she means sex, but she means both sex and firewood. This miscommunication alludes to how transactional the relationships between men and women were in the postwar years. Left without much money or resources, many women had no other choice but to exchange sex for goods. And when Maria so easily chooses Hermann over Bill, one wonders whether her relationship with Bill was just as transactional.

We get our first glimpse of what postwar life has been like when the opening credits fade to white and transition to a scene in the apartment that Maria shares with her mother and her friend Betti (Fig. 14). In this scene, and throughout the film, the set and the decor play an important role. As mentioned earlier, in the first half of the film, Fassbinder frequently uses carefully placed photos of Hermann to convey how the family feels toward him. At the very beginning of the film, there is a black-and-white photo of Hermann in civilian

Figure 14. Maria's mother in their apartment, framed by walls damaged by bombs.

clothing, framed from the shoulders up, placed next to a plate of bread. Later on, when Maria returns from a trip to the black market and longingly stares at Hermann's photo in a shot/reverse shot, the audience will have an inkling that Hermann has either fallen or is a prisoner of war. But in this first scene inside their apartment, right before the close-up of Hermann's photo, we get a close-up of Maria's mother pouring water over a piece of bread (see Fig. 6). Her actions suggest that the bread is stale and the water is needed to soften it. These brief close-ups of Hermann's photo and of the bread speak volumes about the family's financial state in the early postwar years. We can tell by the shabby state of the apartment and the limited food that money is tight and the family must do whatever possible to stretch their resources. Their apartment is dark and shabby and there are gaping holes in the walls, damage from the war. When Maria enters the scene, she is wearing a backpack filled with broken pieces of wood, indicating that she has been scavenging for firewood. She has just returned from the black market, where she has bartered her wedding dress. Thus, her wedding bliss has quickly given way to a state of poverty and living as a presumed widow. Maria quips that it was difficult to sell her dress because "There are too many brides and too few men."

Following the very first scene of Maria and her mother in the kitchen, the film transitions to a shot of Maria at the train station, with other potential war widows, wearing a sandwich-board sign with a black-and-white photo of Hermann in his military uniform and the message "Who knows Hermann Braun? Last message from the area of Smolensk, military postal service number 16310-342" (Fig. 15). She then consults a list of the fallen to see whether Hermann's name is included. After searching in vain for Hermann's name, Maria returns to the entrance of the station. In front of her, a soldier limps along on crutches, missing his left arm (Fig. 16). Maria turns to a German Red Cross nurse and confesses, "I feel sick at the sight of them." She and the nurse confide to each other how

Figure 15. Maria searches for Hermann at the train station while wearing a sandwich board sign with his photo.

unappealing these injured, battered German men appear to them, like Grandpa Berger, whose skinny frame disappears into her dead father's old suit. As Maria's mother later remarks, the men that are left have all shrunk. The motif that German men are disappointing is repeated throughout the first scenes of the film and establishes a basis for Maria's later interest in the African American soldier Bill. This motif is picked up again, for example, when Maria and Betti witness a conflict on the street: a man tries to steal wood from a fence in order to repurpose it as firewood, but two young boys manage to scare him off. Meanwhile, in the background, *Trümmerfrauen* are busy at work while watching the scene from a distance. This sums up the situation of postwar Germany for Maria: there are women hard at work, but the men are weak. She laments to Betti, "something has to happen," a statement that introduces the prospect that Maria will eventually enter into a relationship with one of the American occupiers.

Figure 16. A disabled veteran limps along on crutches, with Maria behind him.

Coca Cola-nization

Evaluating the presence of the American military in Germany from 1945 until 2002, Maria Höhn writes that since the conclusion of World War II, more than fifteen million Americans have lived in West Germany, the majority of whom belonged to the military.[66] Initially, fraternization between the US military and Germans was not only discouraged but illegal. However, in October 1945, the ban on fraternization was lifted. The US Army turned a blind eye towards sexual encounters, but it still sponsored campaigns warning its soldiers to avoid romantic encounters with German women. Höhn argues that the reasons behind these campaigns ranged from sexual health (stopping the spread of venereal disease among soldiers) to ideology (limiting fraternization between soldiers and the "occupied"). One can easily apply Höhn's argument to *A Foreign Affair* (1947), the first feature film that the Austrian Jewish émigré Billy Wilder directed in Germany (having fled Europe for Hollywood in 1933 to escape the Nazis). In this romantic comedy, an

American officer, Captain John Pringle, is caught in a love triangle between a German cabaret singer, Erika von Schlütow, played by Marlene Dietrich, and a member of Congress visiting from Iowa, Phoebe Frost. Throughout the film Wilder conveys that while the US Army and government encourage American GIs to focus on their duties in Germany rather than fraternizing with women, the bored American soldiers would much rather do the opposite. In his analysis of the film, Gerd Gemünden describes Frost as "a symbol for stability and steadfastness, including puritan virtues and political incorruptibility," in contrast to von Schlütow, who is presented as "a femme fatale with a past, only in this tale that past has not only sexual but also political connotations."[67] Initially, Wilder makes Frost the butt of the joke by depicting her as an uptight (communicated by her name), humorless alternative to the sultry, sexy Schlütow. By the end of the film, however, Schlütow confirms the stereotype of the "dangerous" German Fräulein. As it turns out, she is a war criminal who formerly associated with Hitler. Captain Pringle's affair with her was in fact just a ruse to arrest her, and in the end the American soldier (Pringle) and the upstanding American woman (Frost) are the ones who really belong together.[68] As scholars like Höhn and Annette Brauerhoch point out, sexism and jingoism were involved in the decision to depict German women who engaged in sexual relationships with American GIs as sex workers—a heavy-handed, ideologically laden understanding that did not account for each women's individual situation and agency.[69]

When American soldiers first conquered Nazi Germany, the mission was, in part, to chasten the local populations: "Germans would be reconditioned so that they would never seek to plunge the world once again into war."[70] This American air of superiority and a paternalistic attitude came together with the antipathy toward Germans brought on by nearly four years of war and reinforced by the US Army's warning that Germany should still be considered dangerous enemy territory. In *Maria Braun*, we witness how

American soldiers' behavior towards Germans is influenced by their negative views when, towards the beginning of the film, Maria and the German Red Cross nurse she encounters while looking for Hermann enter the train station and have a run-in with a white American soldier. In the station, an assortment of German refugees, returning soldiers, and American GIs sit around tables. Another Red Cross nurse doles out cups of soup to the needy; a disabled veteran hobbles past on crutches. Meanwhile, the nurse speaking to Maria gives a harrowing account of what happened to her own husband during the war: how he braved the gravest of difficulties to return to her and ultimately died "so that Germany could live." Towards the end of the nurse's account, we get an extreme close-up of a white GI with his back to the camera, smoking a cigarette (Fig. 17). When the GI tosses his cigarette on the floor and turns around to face Maria (and therefore the camera), his uniform, black-rimmed glasses, and the casual way he is smoking a cigarette all indicate that he is American; the low camera angle conveys his contempt as he looks down at the German men scrambling for his cigarette butt (Fig. 18).

Figure 17. An American soldier, smoking a cigarette, is seen from behind.

Figure 18. The soldier looks down at Germans fighting over his cigarette.

In the previous shot, the extreme close-up of his ear, the cloud of smoke he exhales, and the fact that we can't see his face all create an ominous feeling (Fig. 17). He is probably eavesdropping on Maria and the nurse. But his curiosity about the lives and struggles of Germans has nothing to do with empathy. It is during a pause in the conversation between Maria and the nurse that he tosses his cigarette over his shoulder onto the ground for some ragged German men to fight over. A cut to a close-up of Maria reveals her observing this scene with pity for the German men and, we will later learn, disdain for the GI, after he says something indecent to her in English. His behavior demonstrates how much disregard the occupying American soldiers have for Germans.

But Maria does not allow herself to be intimidated. She chastises the GI in German for his indecent remark and, in response, he apologizes and gives her a pack of cigarettes to make it up to her. Thus, we see early on that Maria is willing to be bold when others are not, and her boldness is rewarded. And this is just the first inkling of how Maria will use her power and femininity to get by in life and, she believes, use men to help her. This scene also relays both the emasculated state of German men and the arrogance of the *white* American soldiers. This arrogance stemmed from the fact that "many American GIs pouring into Germany shared … deep repugnance toward civilians who appeared altogether too well fed and insufficiently contrite."[71] This repugnance was no doubt only further deepened by the remnants of the Nazi past that were visible in everyday life. In *Maria Braun*, for example, on the wall of the train station the following words are written: "Räder müssen rollen für den …" (Wheels must roll for the …)—with the final word, "Sieg" (victory), scratched out, according to the script.[72] The erasure of the word *Sieg* is an ironic gesture pointing out the diametrically opposite outcome Germany has experienced.

According to German eyewitness accounts, Black American soldiers, in contrast to this disdainful treatment by white Americans, were quite friendly to Germans, often giving children chocolate and chewing gum. Moritz Ege, Andrew Wright Hurley, and Sydney Portal write: "in today's popular iconography, images of friendly African American soldiers passing out chewing gum to children stand as metonyms for the entire era, but what is less often said is that such images implicitly gained their meaning and heft from the stark contrast with Nazi propaganda of 'savage' black rapists."[73] As Timothy Schroer points out, there was much less animosity between African Americans and Germans as compared to the Black French colonial soldiers' attitude towards Germans. African Americans tended to be less hostile towards Germans because they were "heavily overrepresented in … non-combat units."[74] Furthermore, Schroer implies that during the occupation of the Rhineland after the First World War, the French were more lenient towards colonial troops' bad behavior because the French "carried fresh memories of atrocities committed by German troops on French soil."[75] Martin Klimke and Maria Höhn argue that part of the reason that Black American soldiers often were kinder towards Germans was because they felt like they had more in common with this downtrodden, occupied people than with *white* Americans. Black soldiers had experienced plenty of racism from their white American peers in the military. While living in occupied Germany, they were viewed by Germans as the "victors," irrespective of their perceived racial difference. Thus, Black American soldiers often felt Germans treated them with more respect than their white compatriots. This is why, as Klimke and Höhn write, many Black American soldiers viewed their time in Germany as "a breath of freedom": "in much of its coverage, the black press depicted postfascist Germany as a sort of 'Shangri-La' or 'racial utopia' where African Americans could enjoy a better life than they could in their own country."[76] Certainly, the facts that in Germany Black American soldiers were on the victorious side and that many white Germans relied on them and respected them contributed to this feeling of "racial utopia." No doubt the abuse that Black GIs faced from their own white fellow soldiers drove this point home even more.

Nevertheless, Fassbinder does not give us much insight into how Bill experiences postwar Germany, even though several representations of postwar Germany from Black soldiers' perspectives already existed long before *Maria Braun*. These perspectives can be found in texts by African American authors, like William Gardner Smith's *Last of the Conquerors* (1948), or even by white German authors, like Wolfgang Koeppen's *Pigeons on the Grass* (1951) or Heinrich Willi's *Gottes zweite Garnitur* (God's Second String, 1962); all three of these novels portray Black GIs who face racism when they try to date white German women. But Fassbinder, strangely, never directly acknowledges this problem. When Maria and Bill begin to date, no one makes any racist remarks about their relationship. But racism is implied in her killing of Bill, because her decision, even if it was a split-second reaction made under pressure, still devalues and dehumanizes Black life. A second example of the racism inherent in West German society is when Maria's doctor remarks that the death of her interracial baby saved them both (Maria and the baby) from tragedy. This remark exposes the racism present in the culture, because the doctor implies that German society would not have accepted an interracial baby, which would have made Maria's life more difficult.

Another example of how racism is touched on in less explicit ways is how Black GIs are treated like second-class citizens in postwar Germany. The bar where Maria works is in an unattractive location and the space is dusty and cluttered, filled with furniture and remnants of the gym. On Maria's first night working at the bar, we get a sense of what a taboo it is for white German women to dance with Black GIs. When the scene begins, the camera's point of view is from Bronski's office, which is separated from the bar by a dark curtain. When Bronski peels back the curtain, we first see three interracial couples—white women and Black men in uniform—slow dancing in soft, blue light (Fig. 19). In the back right corner sits Bill. In the background, Glenn Miller's "Moonlight Serenade" (1944) plays; a reference to jazz's popularity in Germany during the

Figure 19. The three interracial couples dancing.

1930s and 40s, despite (and in some cases in rebellion against) the Nazis' strictures on Black music. The Nazis had tried, in vain, to restrict the presence of jazz in the Third Reich. But when banning Black and Jewish performers wasn't enough to fight its popularity, they simply coopted the genre, making their own jazz in a form that was acceptable to the Reichskulturministerium (Reich Culture Ministry).[77] During the war, the Allies used the popularity of jazz to try and influence Germans. Miller's "In the Mood" was one of several of his recordings that were broadcast to German troops on a propaganda radio station created specifically for the war.[78] Intermixed with jazz recordings, the bandleader "address[ed] German soldiers in German while extolling the virtues of American life."[79] Even after the war, jazz played an important role in representing the allure of American culture: the "jazz, rock and roll, flashy cars, and consumer riches that the Americans offered, and the younger generation eagerly embraced."[80]

One night while she is working at the bar, Maria sits on a barstool, while she and the female bartender Vevi engage in a contentious discussion about love; one that mirrors similar conversations Maria has had with her mother and with the Red Cross nurse. Maria continues to cling to an ideal of love, insisting that love is something real and true, while Vevi focuses on the material, stating that the only truth she knows is hunger and the only thing she can feel is "between [her] legs." Vevi advises Maria that rather than pining for Hermann, she should focus on a man who's actually there; while she says this, Vevi gestures towards Bill, remarking that he isn't hungry and he is clearly interested in Maria. Vevi states, "He looks healthy and strong. So what if he's black," which is one of the few explicit references to race in the film. To which Maria responds, "better black than brown." This statement not only suggests that Maria has no aversion to dating a Black man, but also that she would prefer dating a Black man to a (former) Nazi: during the 1920s, as the Nazis tried to establish power, the SA wore brown shirts and were

Figure 20. Maria turns around to look at Bill after Vevi suggests he would be a good replacement for Hermann.

referred to as the *Braunhemden*.[81] "Brown" could of course also be a reference to Maria's husband, since his last name, "Braun," is the German word for "brown"—in other words, her answer suggests not only that Bill would be preferable to a former Nazi, but also that she might prefer Bill to Hermann. The fact that Maria later asks Bill to dance, rather than the other way around, reinforces her character as an independent woman who doesn't conform to gender conventions.

Although initially Maria is only open to a friendship with Bill, the two grow closer as they increasingly spend time together. This brief scene in the bar cuts to them taking a stroll in a park one day. During their stroll, we also see how Bill is not only instructing Maria in English, but is also helping her better understand American racial categories, which will be useful information for her in navigating postwar Germany. Bill points out different objects, teaching Maria the words for them in English. Maria repeats Bill's statements word for word. Thus, when he states "I am Black, you are white," Maria repeats these lines verbatim, too; resulting in Maria adopting a Black identity in an unintended linguistic "ethnic drag."[82] Bill laughs, instructing her to reverse the phrases. Maria's unintentional adoption of a Black identity, albeit by mistake, indicates that not only does she not share the beliefs of racist white Germans, but that she may even identify with Blacks. This identification, however, is only superficial, and Maria will abandon it as soon as it's no longer convenient.

In the shooting script, the screenwriters included several scenes that emphasized that Maria was not like racist white Germans of her day, but Fassbinder chose not to include those scenes in the film. For example, in the script, during Maria and Bill's stroll in the park, "an elderly couple [sits] down on a nearby bench and are watching the alleged flirting with disapproval."[83] The woman then says under her breath: "American lover. N***** whore."[84] In another scene that was removed from the shooting script, when Maria first visits the doctor there are several women in the waiting room, and one woman "tells a racist 'dirty joke' about a white woman and a black man. All the women laugh except Maria."[85]

Another scene that was cut had Bill giving Maria numerous gifts that he announces out loud: coffee, chocolate, and nylon stockings. In the film, we only get an inkling of the transactional relationship between Bill and Maria by seeing how her relatives' lives and access to material goods have improved since she met him. This point, that their relationship benefits the entire family, will be emphasized when Maria is on trial for killing Bill and none of her relatives stand up for her, besides Hermann. Thus, Fassbinder demonstrates how Maria's loved ones quickly shun her when she is punished by society.

In the film sequence of their stroll in the park, following several shot/reverse shots of Maria and Bill talking to each other, we get a long shot of the two of them standing in the forest. Although they have not yet become lovers, this setting still resembles a kind of *locus amoenus* where their feelings for each other can presumably grow out of sight from disapproving eyes. This shot appears to

Figure 21. A long shot of Maria and Bill walking in the woods.

be filmed from within a building—an example of Fassbinder's unorthodox camera positions; on the edges, we see the outlines of a broken window (Fig. 21). Thus the shot creates an incidence of internal framing and a perspective not attached to any characters, just one of several such shots of Maria and Bill throughout the film. These shots could be viewed as voyeuristic, implying that someone is watching the couple during their stroll, which would reinforce the notion that Maria and Bill's relationship, though it still hasn't become something sexual, is unconventional, perhaps even transgressive, and would therefore invite the stares of onlookers. When Bill leans behind Maria, presumably to give her a peck on the cheek, his head disappears behind her; this foreshadows the fact that once Maria has what she needs from Bill, namely English skills and more security for her family, she will eventually eliminate him, sacrificing his life for her marriage to Hermann. That Bill and Maria's romance, once it begins, will end tragically, is also foreshadowed by the scene's closing: a fade to black, as ominous, dramatic music plays in the background.

Intersectionality

While scholarship on the film has discussed the importance of Maria's gender and how transgressive it is for her to have an affair with a Black man, scholars and critics alike have said little about the fact that Maria is also complicit in racism and white patriarchy. In fact, in a contemporaneous review of the film, Volker Baer even positions Maria as a victim when she kills Bill. He describes Maria as

> the girlfriend of a Black American soldier who, according to the customs of the time, takes care of her. When she is once again preparing to give herself to him gratefully, her husband, having just returned, appears and stands in the doorway, surprising them both. Out of helplessness, Maria grabs a bottle, with which she hits her lover over the head.[86]

Not only does Baer make Maria out to be a victim despite her act of killing Bill, but his description of their relationship makes it sound like sex work rather than love. In fact, some reviews described Bill's death in the passive voice, which doesn't even make it clear that Maria kills him. Jeffrey Lyon, for example, states: "She's [Maria's] taken up, as they say, with a black American sergeant, and eventually he is killed."[87] In this connection it is interesting to note that in the exposé written by Fassbinder and Raab, Bill's death sounds more like an accident:

> After a short while the door opens, the two of them [Bill and Maria] are terrified. [Hermann], her husband, is standing in front of them, torn and emaciated. [Hermann] throws himself at Bill, who can only with difficulty free himself from his grip, a ruthless fight ensues between the two, and Maria, who wants to protect both at the same time, but also wants to defend each one from the other, hits them with all sorts of accessible objects around her. Suddenly Bill breaks

down, rattling, a pool of blood forms beside his head, blood comes out of his mouth.[88]

Thus, the fact that Fassbinder chose to make Maria's assault on Bill so obviously an intentional act, even though it transpires in the heat of the moment, means he wanted to make Maria's actions all the more morally questionable. Yet still, even in a more recent review, Constance Gorfinkle makes Bill out to be the bad guy who was allegedly taking advantage of Maria.[89] Such negative characterizations are common when it comes to interracial romances between Black men and white women throughout German history. When critics describe their relationship in terms of prostitution, suggesting Maria only gives herself to him in exchange for goods, not because she loves him, this assumption that white German women never willingly engage in sexual relationships with Black men recalls "Die Schwarze Schmach" (The Black Shame), a racist propaganda campaign against the French occupation of the Rhineland following World War I. During their occupation, the French deployed Black colonial troops from as far away as Senegal, Madagascar, and Algeria. These troops were purported to often have relationships with local white German women, and some evidence of consensual relationships does exist (see Fig. 22).

In response to the Black soldiers' presence, white Germans warned that if these soldiers were allowed to police them it would challenge white supremacy, because Black soldiers would be accepted as equals, if not superior, to white men. White Germans also alleged that Black soldiers were raping local women and that, therefore, the Black soldiers' presence would contaminate the blood of Germany and ruin the country.[90] One example of this campaign is the poster in Fig. 23, showing a French colonial soldier, depicted larger than life, sitting on a German landscape made to look female. Thus, in the landscape we see hills, but they also appear to be white breasts. The soldier is drawn as a caricature, in a manner that resembles blackface,

Figure 22. A French colonial soldier posing for a photo with two German women. Source: Stadtarchiv Mainz BPSF/8904 17.

with exaggerated physical features, including large red lips. His position, towering over a feminized German landscape, alludes to the allegations of rape against Black soldiers.[91]

By emphasizing that one must consider the intersections of gender, sexuality, class and race in order to understand *Maria Braun*, I am building on the scholarship of Ingeborg Majer O'Sickey, who describes Hermann's return and Maria's killing of Bill on his behalf as pointing to "institutionalized discourse in both [the US and Germany] that regard a black man's life as less valuable than a white man's."[92] It is easier to adopt a more critical stance towards the idea

Figure 23. A propaganda poster reads "Protest of German women against the colored occupation on the Rhine." Source: Deutsches Historisches Museum.

of Maria as an oppressed white woman when one contextualizes the film within Fassbinder's portrayal of Black masculinity and his fetishization of Black men throughout his career. There are several Black male characters in Fassbinder's films, such as the many roles played by Günther Kaufmann. Kaufmann (1947–2012) was a Black German actor, born to a white German woman who had been in a relationship with a Black GI. Although Kaufmann never knew his biological father, who left Germany before he was born, in Fassbinder's films Kaufmann frequently played the role of a Black GI, such as his role as "Lonely Richard" in *Maria Braun* and a drug-dealing GI in *The Longing of Veronika Voss*. Additional roles that Kaufmann played were a slave in *Whity* (1970) and a queer bar owner in *Querelle*.[93] Another Black actor Fassbinder cast was El Hedi ben Salem, who became famous for the role of a Moroccan guest worker in *Fear Eats the Soul*. Salem also played small roles in ten further films, most notably *The Merchant of Four Seasons* (1971), *World on a Wire* (1973), and *Fox and His Friends* (1975). Fassbinder's tumultuous relationship with Salem, who was first employed as his production assistant, is well-documented in the documentary film *Ali in Paradise* (2011), directed by Viola Shafik. Through a series of interviews with Shafik, several of Fassbinder's former colleagues and friends recall the course of his relationship with Salem, while Salem's family provide a counternarrative, filling in the gaps about Salem's life before and after he met Fassbinder.

Salem was born in Morocco in 1935, and in 1963 he left with his nephew Ahmed to work in France. In *Ali in Paradise*, his nephew claims that they were at a café together in Paris when they first met Fassbinder. By contrast, confidants of Fassbinder's including Ingrid Caven and Rudolf Waldemar Brem, claim that Fassbinder met Salem while cruising at a sauna. In any case, when Fassbinder later met Caven for dinner, he introduced her to Salem and announced that he was taking him back to Germany. Fassbinder would later recreate a scenario of encountering Salem while cruising in the film *Fox and His Friends*, in which the title character Fox (Fassbinder) and his lover Eugen (Peter Chatel) attempt to pick up a Moroccan sex worker (Salem). Fox and Eugen evaluate the sex worker's physical attributes, much like white buyers at a slave auction, and decide to take him back to their hotel room. However, their plans are thwarted when a hotel employee informs them that "Arabs" are not allowed in the hotel. Ironically, Fox and Eugen, who had just been treating

Salem's character as an exotic sexual object, become upset by the hotel's racist policies.

During their romantic relationship, Fassbinder even insisted on bringing two of Salem's sons from Morocco and wanted to serve as a father figure for them. But the boys ended up moving in with Fassbinder's associates Kurt Raab and Hans Hirschmüller instead. (Raab acted in several of Fassbinder's films and also worked for Fassbinder as a production designer, assistant director, producer, and a screenwriter. Hirschmüller acted in *Katzelmacher* and *The Merchant of Four Seasons*.) While Raab could not be interviewed for Shafik's documentary—he died of AIDS in 1988—Hirschmüller does appear, and suggests that one of Salem's sons was sexually abused by Raab. In Shafik's documentary, Fassbinder's contemporaries claim that Fassbinder intended the starring role in *Fear Eats the Soul* to be a monument to Salem. Nevertheless, shortly after the film was made, Fassbinder grew tired of his relationship with Salem, moving on to enter a relationship with Armin Meier, a white, working-class German butcher. After being involved in a knife fight, Salem eventually had to flee Germany; in France, he ended up in jail, where he hung himself in 1977.

While Fassbinder's romantic relationship with Salem is well-documented, his relationship with Kaufmann is shrouded in mystery. On the one hand, Kaufmann is rumored to have been one of Fassbinder's lovers. On the other hand, in his autobiography *Der weisse Neger vom Hasenbergl* (The White Negro of Hasenbergl, 2004), Kaufmann denies having had any romantic or sexual relationship with Fassbinder. He claims that the director was attracted to him early on in their professional relationship—they met when Kaufmann played a role in Volker Schlöndorff's staging of *Baal* in 1969—and that Fassbinder gave him privileged treatment compared to the other actors in the Anti-Theater.[94] Kaufmann recalls that during the shooting of *Whity*, Fassbinder planned for the two of them to share a hotel room, giving him the opportunity to make advances toward Kaufmann. Kaufmann writes candidly of several instances when Fassbinder forced him into intimate scenarios with the threat that, otherwise, he would replace him with someone else. Kaufmann suggests that he was fully aware of Fassbinder's desire for him and exploited it in order to get more roles. Simultaneously, Fassbinder also exploited Kaufmann, who had had no acting experience prior to his involvement in theater. If Kaufmann rejected his romantic advances, Fassbinder could hinder Kaufmann's rise as a star just as easily as he had been propelling it.

It is worth asking whether Fassbinder employed racialized, inexperienced actors like Kaufmann and Salem so he could satisfy his personal desires. Or was his employment of these actors merely linked to his greater interest in marginal characters? Christian Braad Thomsen claims that Fassbinder thought "he could atone for society's abuse of these outsiders and in his films pull them from the edge of society and into the limelight and turn them into film stars."[95] But Fassbinder clearly had his own selfish reasons as well.

Citing Thomsen, Tobias Nagl and Janelle Blankenship point out that Fassbinder's lovers, Kaufmann, Salem, and Meier, were men "who all shared an underprivileged racial or social background in comparison to Fassbinder's upper-middle class upbringing."[96] Thus, despite Meier's whiteness, Fassbinder may have seen him as comparable to Kaufmann and Salem in terms of their overall positions in society. In fact, during a particularly tumultuous period in their relationship, Fassbinder allegedly used his well-known attraction to Black men to make Meier jealous. Meier died by suicide in 1978. During a work trip that Fassbinder took earlier that year, which included stops in New York and Cannes, he flaunted his sexual activities while he was abroad, aggravating the relationship problems he and Meier were experiencing. From Cannes, Fassbinder wrote to Meier: "I'm in Cannes, with a N****r."[97] The person to whom Fassbinder was referring, using the N-word, was a Black bodyguard he had hired for the event. Fassbinder's choice of words is a marker of an accepted anti-Black racism that was widespread in West German society at this time; several of the reviews of *Maria Braun* when it was released referred to Bill in the same way. Even in the cast of characters included in Fassbinder's script, Bill is listed as "N***** Bill," which would suggest that Fassbinder didn't treat the actor with the same respect as the other white actors whose names are actually listed.[98] Given the context of Fassbinder's personal relationships with Black men, it is not at all surprising that, both in his private life and in his films, he viewed them as sexual objects, and assumed that their hypersexual reputation alone was enough to make someone jealous.

In *Maria Braun*, Bill is played by George Byrd (1926–2010), who was also not a trained actor, but an orchestral conductor, one of many African American classical musicians who pursued a career in Germany.[99] Little has been written about Byrd in the secondary literature about the film. Byrd was born in Anson County, North Carolina. He was trained at Juilliard, and in 1951, a month after graduating, he left for Europe, where he settled permanently, only occasionally returning to the United States to conduct.[100] Though his permanent home was Germany, he also served as a guest conductor for orchestras in France, Belgium, Switzerland, England, Denmark, Norway, Sweden, Poland, and Yugoslavia.[101] Although Byrd never got a permanent position in Europe, he still felt that even temporary employment as a conductor would never have been possible in the US. In the late 1960s, Byrd said: "My continued wish is that America would offer me the opportunities Europe has."[102] This is a sentiment that Byrd shares with the World War II-era African American soldiers who served in Germany. In fact, Byrd himself had also served in the US Army. According to his account, he was able to move to Europe with the help of the GI bill: "I went abroad with two letters of recommendation, six months of study available under the G.I. bill and $100. I stayed two years, came back to get my winter clothes and then went back to Europe to stay 17 years."[103]

There are no written accounts of how Byrd and Fassbinder met, making his relationship with the director quite different from that of the other two Black actors—Kaufmann and Salem—whom Fassbinder cast in many more films. Byrd, however, did live in the same neighborhood as Fassbinder in Munich,[104] so perhaps the director had seen him before on the street. According to Sonja Spirk, a former student of Byrd's who later became his friend and eventual caretaker, Byrd got into acting through his friendship with Burt Lancaster (Fig. 24).[105]

Lancaster had been in Munich filming *Twilight's Last Gleaming* (1977), a West German-US coproduction. The film, which was loosely based on the novel *Viper Three* (1971) by Walter Wager, reflected the political tensions of the Cold War. Lancaster played Lawrence Dell, a US Air Force general who served during Vietnam and was a POW there. His experiences in Vietnam have made

Figure 24. Burt Lancaster and George Byrd. Courtesy of Sonja Spirk, private collection.

Figure 25. Byrd in costume on the set of *Twilight's Last Gleaming*. Courtesy of Sonja Spirk, private collection.

him critical of the US military, and he insists that the American government must come clean about its actions during the war. Because of his stance on Vietnam, Dell is viewed as a liability by his superiors, who frame him for manslaughter and send him to prison. Dell escapes prison and takes over an intercontinental ballistic missile silo, threatening to launch the intercontinental ballistic missiles if the president doesn't reveal a secret document about the war to the American people. Byrd told Lancaster that he had been having money trouble because it was difficult for a Black conductor to find long-term work in Europe. Because of Byrd's challenges with employment, Lancaster offered him a small role in the film as an American soldier, which Byrd accepted but which was ultimately cut from the film (Fig. 25).

A year after *Twilight's Last Gleaming* was filmed, someone from the production of *Maria Braun* found Byrd in an index of German actors and offered him the role of Bill. Byrd took the role because he needed the money. After *Maria Braun*, Byrd's only film credit is for an appearance in the comedy *Warten auf Beethoven* (Waiting for Beethoven, 1985/6), where he is named as "George Eagles," which may have been a pseudonym he used.[106] Byrd continued to earn money by teaching and conducting, occasionally did translations, and even worked in eldercare. He never married, but he did father one son, Vincent Byrd Le Sage, with a French woman. (Today, Le Sage is an actor in his own right, with a long list of French acting credits.) George Byrd passed away in Munich in 2010 from heart disease and diabetes.

According to Sonja Spirk, Byrd's friend and carer, after the success of *Maria Braun*, people occasionally recognized him on the street in Germany, but his fame was a double-edged sword: he lost some music jobs because he had appeared nude in the film.[107] The manner in which Byrd's body is put on display in *Maria Braun* underscores Fassbinder's frequent hypersexualization of Black men, making both Maria and Fassbinder complicit in exploiting Black men for their own advantage. In several scenes, although Maria is the female lead, Bill is feminized, due to his racialized position, such as the way she takes charge when she approaches Bill after learning of Hermann's (supposed) death. News of Hermann's passing was delivered by her friend Betti's husband, Willi, after he returns from his time as a POW. After hearing the news from Willi, Maria runs from the house, distraught, heading for the bar where she works. Presumably, she is running to Bill because she needs to be comforted. The film then cuts to her in the bar, walking past several dozen couples dancing to Glenn Miller's foxtrot "In the Mood" (1939), which, like "Moonlight Serenade," had been played during the war as part of the Allies' propaganda efforts.[108] The track is an appropriate choice, for its title conveys that Maria is "in the mood" to have an affair with Bill, while the song's legacy as an American big band classic suggests that Maria's love affair with Bill can be understood within a historical trajectory of Germans seeking escapism in American popular culture. A tracking shot follows her, finally revealing Bill from behind, sitting at a table as Maria approaches (Fig. 26).

Typically, in a scene such as this, the male character would approach the female character and ask her to dance. And in the original exposé on which the film is based, Bill is given more agency, actively pursuing Maria after she learns of Hermann's death: "she returns to working in the bar and tells Bill about the news and the days that followed. Bill is kinder than ever to her and tries to comfort her in his own way. Maria is ready to give in to his renewed request. They meet after work, Bill is waiting for her on the street, they go to her house, where they make love passionately."[109]

But in Fassbinder's film, Maria Braun is the one with agency. She approaches Bill and asks if *he* wants to dance. This public display of romantic interest contrasts with the way their friendship

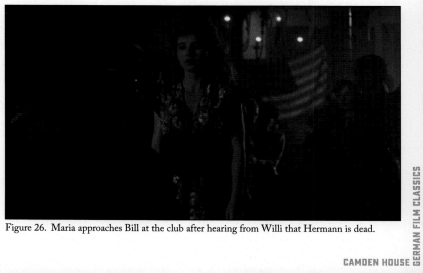

Figure 26. Maria approaches Bill at the club after hearing from Willi that Hermann is dead.

Figure 27. Bill and Maria embrace as she tells him "My man is dead."

was hidden away in the woods in a previous scene. Bill stands and embraces Maria, and she confesses to him, in English: "My man is dead" (Fig. 27). Presumably, this is a linguistic mistake. Maria might mean "husband": in German, the word for both "man" and "husband" is *Mann*, making this an easy mistake for a German-speaker to make in English. However, by saying "my man is dead" instead of "my husband is dead," the line may also suggest that rather than a replacement husband for Maria, Bill is merely a distraction; he is an object. This may be why, prior to going to the bar, Maria announces to her mother that she needs to be alone. If being with Bill is equivalent to being alone, Maria may not even recognize him as a full subject, because she is merely using him. The scene closes with Glenn Miller's "Sunrise Serenade"; a new day is dawning in Maria's life, now that she is certain Hermann is dead.

Bill is also feminized during the first sex scene between the two, because of how his body is displayed. In her foundational essay, "Visual Pleasure and Narrative Cinema," Laura Mulvey insists on the usefulness of psychoanalysis for analyzing cinema, by describing how in film the act of looking vs. being looked at is typically organized according to a gender binary. Mulvey writes:

> In a world ordered by sexual imbalance, pleasure in looking has been split between active/male and passive/female. The determining male gaze projects its phantasy onto the female figure which is styled accordingly. In their traditional exhibitionist role women are simultaneously looked at and displayed, with their experience coded for strong visual and erotic impact so that they can be said to connote *to-be-looked-at-ness*.[110]

But in *Maria Braun*, during Maria and Bill's first intimate moment together, it is Bill who is put on display for the audience. The scene begins with an extreme close-up, focusing on Bill's left shoulder. He is positioned lying on his right side, looking down at Maria, but aside from her hand wrapped around Bill's back, Maria is completely excluded from the frame (Fig. 28).

Figure 28. Maria and Bill in bed.

Figure 29. Maria caresses a nude Bill.

What is also remarkable in this first shot is that Bill is covered in droplets of sweat. The dark lighting casts shadows on his nude body, making him appear even darker than usual. Without a clear shot of Maria's face, our only indications that she is the woman in this scene with Bill are her voice and her manicured hand, which strokes his torso and arm. Her wedding ring is prominently displayed in the shot, a reminder to us that despite Maria's belief that Hermann is dead, there is still a chance he might ruin this affair.

After Maria's hand caresses Bill's naked torso, the scene quickly cuts to an extreme close-up of Maria's naked backside as she lies on her stomach. Like Bill's, her body is also covered in sweat. Now his hand caresses her. In a third shot (Fig. 29), Bill appears to be lying on his back, while Maria caresses his stomach. His left leg is bent and placed on the bed in such a way that his penis is hidden from view. But the shot is nevertheless rather risqué, as we get an extreme close-up of his belly and his leg. Rather than a continuous shot in this scene, we are given a montage of the lovers in different positions, but we don't actually see them move around. Their movement is simply implied: the scene begins with Bill bent over Maria and ends with Maria leaning over him, an indication of the power relations between them, which will end with Maria having the upper hand. In fact, at the end of this scene, Bill proposes marriage to Maria and she turns him down, stating: "I'm very fond of you and I want to be with you, but I'll never marry you."

This scene stands out not only because of its depiction of an interracial couple and the ways in which both Bill and Maria become objects of the camera's gaze, but also because of Bill's body type, which departs from conventional beauty norms, as at least one German reviewer emphasized, describing Bill as a "fat, good-natured, black giant."[111] This description makes it clear how some reviewers objectified Bill, focusing on his physical difference, whether that be his race or his weight. It also plays into the image that white Germans had of Black GIs following the war.

Because Fassbinder edited the first sex scene as a montage rather than a more fluid scene, we never see Maria or Bill completely naked, just parts of them; this changes in a subsequent scene, however, when Maria kills Bill as he stands naked with his back to her. Thus, rather than attempting to shield Bill's racialized nudity from the audience altogether, Fassbinder may simply have been teasing us with intimate shots of him before the later ultimate reveal. This first sex scene with Bill contrasts starkly with the later scene in which Maria and her lover Oswald first sleep together. The latter scene (Fig. 30) is shot in dark, blue tones, creating many shadows and making it difficult to see clearly. Rather than both lovers in the nude, we only see Maria naked, lying face down. The only part of Oswald's body we see is an extreme close-up of his hand, as he caresses Maria from her backside to her shoulder. And while she is completely naked, we can see that he is wearing a robe. There is a lot less intimacy in this scene, because not only is Maria lying face down, but she appears to be turned away from Oswald, not looking at him. This is nothing like the scenes of passion we saw earlier between her and Bill.

Figure 30. Maria and Oswald in bed.

The Melodrama of Race

Though Linda Williams calls melodramas about race an American mode, one could argue that Germans have been just as inclined to use melodrama to discuss racial conflict in society. Just like in the US, white Germans have, at least since the nineteenth century, feared miscegenation and worried that "inferior races" would "replace" them. This type of paranoia around miscegenation can be traced back to the colonial period, when Germany counted several African territories among its colonies, including German Southwest Africa, German East Africa, Cameroon, and Togo. In 1905, a law was passed in German Southwest Africa that banned marriages between German men and African women. An amended law not only retroactively voided previously legal marriages, but also "stripped wives and children of their German citizenship, making all children of these unions 'bastards' and subject to the laws governing the native population."[112] To combat the "problem" of white men marrying Black women, German politicians encouraged white

German women to resettle to the colonies. Furthermore, the desire to protect white *women* from Black *men* is particularly evident from the "Black Shame on the Rhine" campaign, mentioned previously. Approximately five hundred Black German children were born in the Rhineland during the occupation, fathered by colonial soldiers. Adolf Hitler even targeted this group of Black German children in *Mein Kampf*, writing: "It was and it is Jews who bring the Negroes into the Rhineland, always with the same secret thought and clear aim of ruining the hated white race by the necessarily resulting bastardization, throwing it down from its cultural and political height, and themselves rising to be its master."[113]

O'Sickey observes that in the film, Maria collaborates "with white male power at the expense of the other,"[114] meaning both Bill and "Lonely Richard." Maria is not only fond of Bill, but both of them share the experience of marginalization. Bill is a Black soldier, in a segregated army, serving in a majority-white country. Maria is a widow, without a formal education, who has to work as a hostess to get by. Nevertheless, Maria reveals her alliance with white supremacy and patriarchy when Hermann returns out of the blue. At the start of this sequence, Maria has just returned from the doctor, where she learned that she's pregnant with Bill's child. Thus, Hermann's return disrupts an otherwise happy moment in Maria and Bill's relationship. Though Bill is disappointed that she turned down his marriage proposal, his spirits are lifted when Maria tells him she's pregnant.

With the plot twist of Maria's pregnancy, Fassbinder draws on yet another major historical moment from the immediate postwar: the thousands of Black German children that were fathered by African American soldiers.[115] As I have noted, there had been a smaller group of Black German children born after World War I, so this was actually the second time in Germany that military occupation involving Black soldiers resulted in the birth of indigenous Black German children. Those children born after World War I were degradingly called "Rhineland bastards," and during the Weimar

Republic plans to force sterilization on them were discussed. The Nazis later carried out such illegal sterilizations in secret.[116]

Thus, in the aftermath of World War II, when Germans were once again confronted with the birth of Black German children, they recalled the Rhineland occupation. However, due to the new political climate of the democratic Federal Republic of Germany, Germans could no longer be overtly racist in their response to the existence of Black German children. Instead, as Heide Fehrenbach argues, previous discussions about racial inferiority, which had been acceptable during Weimar and Nazi Germany, were reformulated to instead express concern over "cultural difference." As a result, the West German press and politicians conveyed concern about the children's prospects in the country. Fehrenbach suggests that American occupation had "introduced to Germans the reigning American social-scientific tool for investigating racism, namely, 'prejudice studies,' which emphasized the psychological costs of racism for victim and society."[117] Thus, Germans felt totally comfortable arguing that Black children could not be happy there, due to a combination of continuing biases as well as an alleged "incompatibility" between Black children and Germany's environment. This psychological approach to race could "easily authorize a policy of social segregation and emigration."[118] Furthermore, many of the mothers of these children were low-income single parents and therefore even more strongly affected than others by the housing shortage immediately after the war. These sociohistorical issues were compounded by the fact that Black German children, as the so-called "illegitimate" children of mothers who were seen as "degenerate," were assumed to have no future, not only because of their mothers' poor financial state but also because of the inherent character flaws they were assumed to possess and the challenges they were expected to face in a racist society.[119]

Most of these Black German children born after World War II were located in southern Germany, which was the main site of the American occupation. The fact that Fassbinder grew up in Munich makes it more likely that he would have encountered numerous Black Germans of this generation, not just Günther Kaufmann. The fate of many of these Black German children was quite tragic. Several books, like Yara-Collete Lemke Muniz de Faria's *Zwischen Fürsorge und Ausgrenzung* (Between Welfare and Exclusion, 2002) and Heide Fehrenbach's *Race after Hitler* (2005), document the treatment many of them faced. More than seven thousand were removed from their families and either put up for adoption abroad or placed in children's homes, where they suffered physical, psychological, and sexual abuse.[120] Those who remained in Germany had to contend with everyday racism, exoticization, fetishization, and discrimination in school and later on the job and housing markets. However, we never see what Maria and Bill's child would have experienced. It appears that Maria chooses to abort the child—after she kills its father following Hermann's return.

At the start of the sequence in which Hermann returns, Maria and Bill enter her apartment building, clearly enthralled with each other, after she has revealed that she is pregnant. Maria leaps into Bill's arms, and he carries her upstairs. This scene, in the building's entryway, is shot from a high angle, with a perspective from the stairs (Fig. 31). Because the camera perspective is not attached to Maria or Bill it creates the illusion that someone is secretly watching them from the stairwell. This cinematography echoes the claustrophobic and judgmental atmosphere that Fassbinder created in *Fear Eats the Soul*, his other film involving interracial romance, which makes great use of shots on staircases and in stairwells. Although we know Maria has refused to marry Bill, this shot of him carrying her in his arms, standing next to the threshold, inevitably recalls two newlyweds. Thus, if the perspective from the stairs implies a disapproving gaze, it could be that of a nosy neighbor or could foreshadow Hermann's return to interrupt their romantic bliss.

The foreshadowing of Hermann's return is also conveyed by the characters' declaration, as they enter, that the apartment is

Figure 31. Bill prepares to carry Maria up the stairs to her apartment.

empty. As we know, Fassbinder likes to undermine his characters'
expectations at every turn. Thus, while they expect to have the
privacy to celebrate the good news of Maria's pregnancy, Hermann
will soon disappoint them. After Bill sets Maria down just beyond
the threshold of the bedroom, he remains in the doorway, his back
towards Maria as he peers over his shoulder into the room (Fig. 32).
It's as if he already knows this will be the end of their relationship.
His physical separation from Maria, at the threshold—the space
of liminality—emphasizes that he will not be accompanying her
on the rest of her journey. The shadows across his face convey an
ominous feeling; they could even be said to resemble the prison
bars that will soon separate Maria from Hermann, after she
murders Bill. Before they reached the doorway, Bill had asked
Maria, "Bist Du guter Hoffnung?" (Are you hopeful?)— which is
a euphemism for "Are you expecting?"—to which Maria answers
in the affirmative. In this context, the phrase has several meanings.
Not only does it confirm that Maria is pregnant, but it also suggests
that she is hopeful for her future, presumably a future with Bill,
which is about to be cut short.

Figure 32. Bill in the doorway to Maria's room, just before Hermann's arrival.

In the bedroom, Maria and Bill banter about how they will raise their child bilingually. They tease each other about who is more attractive, German women or American women, and German men or American men. All of this pillow talk happens as Maria undresses Bill, in the righthand corner of the frame. Bill's statement that "German men are ugly" directly precedes Hermann appearing in the doorway, in the far left of the frame (Fig. 33).

At first, neither Maria, who has her back to the door, nor Bill notices Hermann. Hermann stands in the doorway, observing the couple like a ghost back from the dead. The pair of lovers continues to trade compliments back and forth as they undress. Maria calls Bill rich, strong, and courageous: all of the things Hermann is not. But despite Bill's structural position as wealthier and physically stronger than most German men at this time, Maria takes on a rather domineering role in this encounter. She pulls down Bill's pants and underwear, leaving him completely exposed before the camera, revealing the corpulent body that Karena Niehoff describes, negatively, as fat.[121] While Bill stands there in the nude, Maria is still wearing a slip and is never completely naked in this scene, which

Figure 33. Hermann appears in the doorway as Maria undresses Bill.

underscores how much more vulnerable Bill is at this moment. Maria pushes Bill down onto the bed before sitting down next to him. These actions reinforce her character as the strong, independent, postwar woman. They also potentially make the scene even more painful for Hermann *and* debunk racist German narratives about the encounters between white German women and African American soldiers. Contrary to the myth of the "Black Shame on the Rhine," it is not Bill who is overpowering Maria and forcing himself on her. She is clearly choosing to be intimate with him—a reality that would potentially strike a blow to the ego of any German soldier returning at this time; this is why, in Maria's mind, Bill must die, as is reflected in the original script, discussed below.

It is Bill who, while he is kissing Maria's shoulder and her back is to the door, finally spots Hermann standing in the doorway. The close-up of Hermann's face, from Bill's point of view, does not look angry or even sad, just resigned. The muted tones of the set make him look pale and tired. Once she notices Hermann, Maria is clearly happy to see him; but when she approaches him joyfully, he slaps her in the face. Maria falls to the ground, overdramatically—another example of the stilted acting that Fassbinder's films are known for. Bill, ever the gentle giant, does not seek revenge against Hermann, but goes to check on Maria instead. Meanwhile, Hermann has caught a glance of the cigarettes on the table, and they are now his primary concern. Seeing Maria with Bill may have hurt his pride, but his current concern is fulfilling base needs and desires: enjoying some kind of immediate gratification after having likely spent some time in a prisoner-of-war camp. Hermann's going for the cigarettes *first* was added to the shooting script by Fassbinder. It represents yet another moment in which the motif of cigarettes as currency arises in the film. A further example of, in Anton Kaes's words, how "the camera emphasizes people's greed for simple pleasures like cigarettes or coffee through frequent, often obtrusive close-ups."[122]

Visually, the characters have now traded places in the frame. Hermann sits alone on the bed, while Maria is still seated on the floor, with Bill crouching over her, both supporting her *and* protecting her. They both stare intently at Hermann, as if they are unsure of what he might do next (Fig. 34). Hermann's anger returns, and he begins ripping up the sheets on the bed. Rather than attack

Figure 34. Maria and Bill wait to see what Hermann will do next.

Hermann, Bill grabs hold of him in order to calm him down and, after Hermann stands up, the two struggle. Hermann eventually gives in, and in a tender moment, he turns his back to Bill, which one can read as a sign of vulnerability, for Hermann allows Bill to embrace him from behind. This scene of interracial masculine empathy and reconciliation is abruptly interrupted when Maria, holding an empty bottle she has picked up from the floor, smashes Bill on the top of the head, resulting in his immediate death as he collapses to the floor. This is yet another moment in the film where reality is suspended; Maria's blow does not seem that hard. Kaes describes Maria as acting "as if in a trance."[123] But the point of this scene is not to be realistic; it is that Maria has made a conscious choice in favor of Hermann instead of Bill. And even if she did not intend to kill Bill, her actions have removed him from the narrative and theoretically cleared a path for her and Hermann to be reunited. In the original script, we get a clearer idea of what motivated Maria's actions. When Bill restrains Hermann, "Maria sees the process, she can no longer bear Hermann's humiliation, takes a bottle from the table and hits Bill over the head. Bill collapses."[124]

Maria may have killed Bill to save her marriage and her husband's pride, but in keeping with the theme of Fassbinder's work, Maria's dream will be deferred. In the next scene, we see Maria in an American military court, standing trial for Bill's murder. The scene is introduced with a shot of an American flag, as the camera tilts down to reveal evidence of the crime: Bill's bloody fatigues and his army boots. In a later shot, the American tribunal sits before the gigantic American flag that hangs from the wall. The presence of the flag is no doubt a reference to Americans' immense power in postwar Germany and their task of denazifying the population. The trial appears quite theatrical; not only are there German actors, with noticeable accents, performing in the role of American soldiers, but their speech in English directed at Maria is then repeated in German by an interpreter, and all of Maria's testimony in German is repeated in English by the same German interpreter. The result is a confusing cacophony of sounds and languages, a confusion only heightened by the fact that a single interpreter is translating for both Maria and the officer interrogating her. Ultimately, the purpose of all this translation may have been to allow for a clear *mistranslation* to take center stage. When an officer questions Maria about her feelings for Bill, her response echoes an earlier scene. She states: "Ich liebe meinen Mann. Bill habe ich lieb gehabt" (I love my husband. I was fond of Bill). The German phrase *lieb haben* is somewhat untranslatable. While the phrase uses the root of the word "love" (*Liebe*), it is best translated as "to be fond of" someone. Thus, when the interpreter states in English, "She loved Bill and she loves her husband," the American officer condescendingly responds: "That is really a very fine difference." Clearly, both the interpreter and the American officer are missing the point. Fassbinder includes this mistranslation to suggest that these men, both German and American, are incapable of understanding Maria's feelings. Maria ultimately *chooses* Hermann. She can "only" be with one man, because presumably neither one would tolerate sharing her, even if she were willing.

Maria's testimony is cold and matter-of-fact. She does not deny meeting Bill in a bar that is off limits to Germans; she smirks when they refer to her as a bar girl, even though they are clearly implying that she is a sex worker—after all, a self-respecting white woman wouldn't have sex with a Black man. In the court scene, the GIs clearly view Maria not as a victim but as an unethical, "egotistical" *Veronika*—a slur used by GIs against "immoral" German women—who let herself be "kept" by Bill; sexist language that, on the one hand, marks Maria as a passive sexual object while, at the same time, also accuses her of "attaching herself" to Bill like a parasite with the intention of exploiting their relationship. The view of German women reflected in this scene is akin to how German women are portrayed in Wilder's *A Foreign Affair*—as untrustworthy and opportunistic. When the tribunal accuses Maria of doing favors for Bill—a euphemism for sex—in exchange for chocolate and stockings, the camera quickly darts around to her loved ones in the audience—giving us close-ups of Betti, Willi, and Maria's mother, because when Maria accepted these things from Bill, she was looking out not just for herself, but for them too. They too benefited from this relationship. They may choose to remain silent during Maria's interrogation, but the dramatic music condemns their actions. This scene contributes to another motif of the film: Maria makes sacrifices for the good of the family only to see her own happiness slip through her fingers, as will soon become evident.

Hermann is present at the trial and, at first, lurks in the background, dressed in clothing that allows him to blend in with the crowd: a fedora, a suit, and an overcoat—which is also the quintessential costume of a male protagonist in *film noir*, a generic reference that Fassbinder frequently uses in his BRD trilogy (even more prominently in *Veronika Voss* than here).[125] This visible reference to *film noir* is fitting, for just as the male characters in those postwar films tended to find themselves in difficult situations at the hands of unscrupulous women, so too will Hermann: he ultimately decides to confess to Bill's murder in order to allow Maria to go free. His only statement at the trial—"I killed the N*****"—evokes not only the racism still present in postwar Germany but also Fassbinder's own racism; as discussed above, he was known to have referred to his Black actors and lovers with the same offensive term.

In a scene from the original script that was left out of the film, the court asks Maria how she reacted to her husband killing Bill:

JUDGE
Ms. Braun, can you tell us how you felt after your husband committed the crime? Like I said, you only have to answer if you want to.

MARIA
I was full of grief. And I felt proud at the same time. Proud and happy.

Excitement in the courtroom. The bailiff calls for order.

JUDGE
Silence please. Mrs. Braun, would you like to explain that to us?

MARIA (*to Hermann*)
I lost a friend. But I knew at that moment that I was loved more than any other woman in the world.[126]

Maria's final statement suggests that the Black man's pain and death is a necessary transaction for proving heterosexual white love.

It is during Maria's first visit to Hermann in jail that Fassbinder sets up Maria's motivations for the rest of the film. Despite Hermann's insistence that Maria should move on with her life and find another man, she vows to wait until he has served his sentence and then "we will begin our life, when we're together again." During this chaotic scene, Maria and Hermann are shouting in order to be able to hear each other over the other two families visiting incarcerated loved ones in the same room. But just before Maria makes her vow, everyone else in the room suddenly falls silent, making her yelling seem excessive. Afterwards, everyone bursts out laughing at Maria's statement—Hermann, Maria, and the other families present. But on the level of narrative, the laughter could also be prompted by the statement itself, not the yelling. Maria may intend for their life together to finally begin once Hermann is released from jail, but this is not what will actually happen. Their life together will be derailed by the desires of her subsequent lover, the industrialist Karl Oswald. The laughter indicates how absurd it is that Maria thinks she knows what her true desires are and thinks she can attain them. The cynicism conveyed in this scene mirrors Fassbinder's remarks in his essay about *Imitation of Life*: "nothing is natural. Ever. Not in the whole film. And yet they are all trying desperately to make their thoughts and desires their own."[127] Maria wants to experience true love, but that desire is at odds with her struggle to achieve a secure position in the social hierarchy.

Economic Wonderwoman

Throughout the film, Fassbinder conveys to us how the lives of Maria and her family improve as Germany gets back on its feet economically. Alongside the inability to mourn, this is a further way in which her life serves as an allegory for the country. Maria can be considered a modern woman, in the vein of second-wave feminism, because she always finds a way to survive on her own terms regardless of what other people think. First, she navigates the black market and barters goods to feed her family. Then, her relationship with Bill gives them increased access to commodities that would otherwise be difficult to acquire. We see the next improvement to the family's status after Maria begins working for Oswald, who owns a textile factory. Because Maria never received career training of any kind, as she confides to Hermann during a prison visit, she has to rely on her newly acquired skill set, namely her knowledge of English. This is one of the reasons Maria catches the eye of Oswald, played by Ivan Desny.

Maria meets Oswald while she's on a train, returning home from a clinic in the Black Forest where she has gone to be treated by her old doctor, who is now living there with his daughter.[128] Maria has either sought out his care because she has miscarried or in order to get an abortion. We don't see the actual doctor's visit, just the doctor accompanying her back to the train station and assuring her that she will be alright. Like many of the politicians of that time, he insists that a Black child would have had a difficult life in Germany. He declares that her child is now a "black angel," a phrasing that also alludes to the euphemism for abortion doctors as "angel makers." Though some scholars argue that for this reason Maria must have aborted the child,[129] in a previous scene she can be seen visiting Hermann in jail, trying to convince him she can raise the child until he gets out. Thus, the narrative is unclear as to whether she aborted the child intentionally. The doctor's remarks, "the Lord giveth, the Lord taketh away," could just as well suggest that she had a miscarriage.

On the train ride home, because the train's coach section is so full of Germans crisscrossing the country, trying to get settled after the war, Maria seeks refuge in a first-class car where the only passenger is Oswald. Prior to entering the train car, Maria asks the conductor to upgrade her ticket to first class. The conductor is the one who informs her that Oswald is sitting in the train car, and that he is French and has a factory in Germany. Upon hearing this, Maria quickly goes into the restroom to change her clothes in order to look more appealing. She recognizes that catching this rich man's eye could be her key to economic security. She emerges with her hair pinned up and wearing pearl earrings and makeup, looking like the poster child for modern, successful womanhood (Fig. 35).

Maria lives by the motto, "fake it till you make it": the embodiment of neoliberal fortitude *avant la lettre*, she will project the kind of success she desires until she is able to actually manifest it, similar to

Figure 35. Framed by the doors of the train car, Maria walks past Oswald and then turns to look back at him.

Imitation of Life's Lora. The conductor's stunned face as he watches her walk down the aisle models the fascination Oswald will soon feel when he encounters her. And by having the conductor bring her suitcase to her after she has sat down across from Oswald, she conveys the image of a woman who is powerful enough to be taken care of, rather than one who is a caretaker. Later that same evening, after Maria has arrived home, Betti even states that looking at Maria, no one would be able to tell what she's been through; this could be read not only as a statement about Maria's character but about 1950s Germany, trying so hard to forget its Nazi past and the chaotic 1940s.

Oswald, whose textile company operates internationally, is in need of a "personal adviser" who speaks English, because he speaks only German and French. His need for someone who speaks English reflects America's new economic and political dominance in the world. English is now the *lingua franca*, and Maria's ability to speak it gives her the means to improve her station in society. Thus, like Lora in *Imitation of Life*, Maria has used her relationship with her Black companion (in Lora's case Annie, in Maria's case Bill) to move up the social totem pole. Maria works her magic on Oswald, acting uninterested in his questions at first. We see this encounter partially from the perspective of the conductor standing at the end of the aisle, outside the half-open compartment doors, within which Oswald and Maria are framed. As is typical for this type of internal framing in Fassbinder's films, one of the implications is that both Maria and Oswald are trapped, but we will have to wait to learn what each of them is trapped by: Maria by her desire for success and Oswald by his desire for love.

Maria is able to put her talents on display when "Lonely Richard" enters the train car and makes a rude pass at her. Lonely Richard, as I noted earlier, is played by Günther Kaufmann (Fig. 36), who would go on to play a similar role in *Veronika Voss* two years later, namely that of a loud, belligerent GI without any backstory. His

Figure 36. Lonely Richard says something "indecent" to Oswald about Maria.

presence in the film is that of a prop, a symbol of America's power in postwar Germany and of the exotic allure of Blackness. Kaufmann's acting in this scene is exaggerated, his dialogue stilted. Although he's supposed to be American, he keeps using the British expression "bloody." He greets Maria and Oswald with "Hello guys and dolls," recalling the musical *Guys and Dolls* (1950) set in 1930s New York and revolving around the criminal underworld. The use of this phrase is another example of Fassbinder's intentional citations of pop culture, reminding viewers that this is an artificial recreation of the past. The behavior of the American soldiers throughout the film gives the impression that for many American soldiers at the time, German women were nothing but potential sexual partners, too desperate to turn down a GI's advances. O'Sickey views this scene as another example of how Fassbinder stereotypes Black men: "the black man as an out-of-control sexual predator who desires and accosts white women"—which, as I have noted, is a stereotype that can be traced back to the Rhineland occupation of the 1920s.[130] But Maria has always been a woman who attempts to control her own destiny, and she quickly rebukes "Lonely Richard" using a few scathing, profane words in English. Oswald is none the wiser; she explains that she chased Richard off by telling him what an important person Oswald was, not that she threatened to kick him until his testicles fell off. Thus, "Lonely Richard," like Bill, is yet another Black man whom Maria can instrumentalize to get what she wants. His interaction with Maria allows her to demonstrate not only her knowledge of English, but also the fact that she is a desirable woman: two things that make her a valuable commodity in Oswald's eyes. And ultimately, Maria's goal is to align herself with power, embodied by Oswald, the older, white, male industrialist.

When Maria and Oswald's paths cross on the train, it presents an opportunity for both characters: Maria finds employment, and Oswald finds an assistant who can speak English. When Oswald introduces Maria to his bookkeeper, Senkenberg (Hark Bohm), she lets them both know that she intends to be the first woman at their company in a top position, an allusion to the changing role of women in West German society. Maria uses her knowledge of English, her poker face, and her good looks to give Oswald a leg up in his negotiations with American companies. She is able to secure a deal that will let Oswald manufacture nylon rather than woven stockings, which can only mean more economic success for the company because nylon was cheaper and more desirable due to its wash-and-wear quality.

In the West Germany of the 1950s, it was mostly single women who were encouraged to get jobs. Married women, by contrast, were encouraged to be housewives. But the reality was that many women, even if they were married, had to work for pay at least part time. When, in the latter half of the film, Betti's husband Willi encounters Maria at a business meeting—he as the representative of union workers and Maria representing Oswald's company—Willi delights in how much Maria has changed. He laments that he is unhappy in his marriage to Betti, saying he needs someone more sophisticated that he can talk to but instead he has Betti, who can only cook for him. Willi admires that Maria is capable of learning. While Betti has remained in her old role of housewife, Maria has evolved into something else. She is a better match for the men of this modern time.

Soon, Maria and Oswald begin a relationship, which provides them relief from their loneliness. The trope of the female assistant who has an affair with her male boss is an old one. But Fassbinder puts his own spin on this plotline by having Maria take the lead in the relationship. Although Maria's mother is worried that Oswald will take advantage of her, it is Maria who, on the eve of their celebrating a win for the company, announces that she'd like to sleep with him. She makes it a point to draw a line between the Maria Braun who wants to sleep with Oswald and the Maria Braun who works for him. It is important to her that she be valued at work for her skills and not for her relationship to him. She wants to be paid for what her work is worth, and not for the worth of her body. Soon, she finds herself in a dilemma with Oswald that is similar to the one she had with Bill: he falls in love with her and wants her to marry him. But although she turns Oswald down flat-out, Maria never reveals the truth about her marriage to Hermann or Hermann's imprisonment. Whenever she visits Hermann in jail, she gives Oswald a vague excuse why she is busy. Maria wants to keep this information from Oswald in order to have the upper hand.[131] This is why Maria insists that Oswald isn't having an affair with her; "in truth, I'm having one with you." It's all about agency. Maria always wants to know who she's dealing with: Oswald the private person or Oswald her boss. Men have a tendency to confuse these things and occupy whatever role happens to give them an advantage. Maria believes the only way for her to remain married *and* simultaneously maintain her agency is to have her husband physically behind bars, to set the parameters for her affair with Oswald, and to have control over her own money.

But all of Maria's scheming can't save her from an unhappy ending, which is foreshadowed when Oswald accompanies Maria to her mother's birthday party. We can see that all of her relatives are clearly much better off now, since the onset of the economic miracle (when, beginning in 1948, the United States lent money to West Germany in the form of the Marshall Plan to help rehabilitate the economy). Maria's money has allowed her mother to assume a new, younger look: she now has her hair dyed and in curls, which has in turn helped her to find a new, younger boyfriend, Hans Wetzel (whom Maria isn't happy about). Reflecting the moral situation of 1950s West Germany, the party is full of decadence, in the form of excessive food and alcohol, but the atmosphere is sad. All the money in the world cannot fill the emptiness each character still carries around. Oswald is ill and knows he doesn't have much longer to live. Towards the end of the party scene, the guests dance to Rudi Schuricke's "Capri Fischer" (1949), another reference to the economic miracle with its setting in Italy reflecting Germans' longing to travel. In the 1950s, Germans were finally wealthy enough to travel south again on vacation, and this became a central theme in their pop music. In "Capri Fischer," Schuricke sings from the perspective of an Italian fisherman who must toil away at sea to earn money and hopes that his love Marie (a name that echoes "Maria") will remain true to him. As the guests dance to the sentimental music of "Capri Fischer," Maria, turning in circles (Fig. 37), changes dance partners, from Willi, to Grandpa Berger, to Hans, and then to her mother, before finally stopping in front of Oswald.

This depiction of Maria as being passed along among ever-changing dance partners recalls the theme of Arthur Schnitzler's controversial play *Reigen* (La Ronde, 1897). In the play, Schnitzler scrutinizes sexual morality by depicting successive encounters between pairs of characters who have been sexually intimate. The title, *Reigen*, refers to a type of round dance that allows participants to change partners. By alluding to both the dance and to Schnitzler's play, Fassbinder

Figure 37. Maria changes dancing partners while "Capri Fischer" plays as diegetic music.

emphasizes the transactional nature of Maria's character. But despite what she believes, Maria is not really in control. Unbeknownst to her, Oswald and Hermann have struck a deal negotiating ownership over her. And this is alluded to in the lyrics of the song. Schuricke sings of "Bella Marie" (beautiful Marie), "I led this life for you. For us," which is similar to what Maria and Hermann say to one another when the two meet again at the end of the film. When the two are finally reunited after Oswald's death, Hermann turns down Maria's savings and the money she inherited from Oswald, because it's her money. Hermann does this even though he was perfectly fine with accepting money directly from Oswald for Maria, who was thereby functioning as an object Hermann was lending to Oswald.

An Explosive Ending

From the very beginning of her relationship with Oswald, Maria is open to Hermann about it, which makes Hermann feel jealous and embarrassed. During one conversation he feels particularly emasculated, because Maria informs him that she has slept with Oswald for the first time. He doesn't want the prison guard to overhear that she's slept with another man, for fear that this will further humiliate him. But Maria maintains the same claim that she made after she murdered Bill: she loves Hermann as her husband, and nothing else should matter. Maria tells Hermann in jail: "It's not a good time for feelings . . . that's why nothing really affects me." Once again, Maria is portrayed here as a stand-in for West Germany, cold and calculating. As long as she is focused on economic success, she isn't able to properly work through her emotions, or even *have* any emotions, for that matter. Fassbinder implies that West Germans were too quick to move on after the war. Just as the Mitscherlichs suggest, Germans did not give themselves time to mourn and were therefore destined to adhere to the same patterns of authoritarian, patriarchal thinking. During this conversation, the sound of the guard playing with his keys is so loud that it interferes with the dialogue. A shot of the guard in shallow focus emphasizes his presence and his fiddling with the keys. Despite all of Maria's efforts to be cold and distant and orchestrate the things in her life, she does not in fact hold the keys to her own happiness. And she will find this out in the end, right before she chooses to die in a passionate explosion rather than be a pawn in a man's game.

The film concludes after Oswald's death and Hermann and Maria's reunion, presumably what we've been waiting for throughout the film, since Hermann had to hurry back to the front after their wedding. Maria is now living in a large house that she has bought with her earnings; she has come a long way from the war-damaged apartment she once shared with her mother. She has just returned from Oswald's funeral when Hermann surprises her by ringing her doorbell. Maria is clearly flustered. She hadn't been expecting Hermann to return yet. After all, Hermann had actually been released from prison several years earlier. But when Maria went to pick him up upon his release, she found that he had already gone. He left a letter for her in which he claimed that he was heading for Australia or Canada, where he could find work and save some money of his own. In order to feel rehabilitated as a man, and like a legitimate head of the household, it was important for Hermann to make his own way. It's no coincidence that the two possible destinations he names are both settler colonies. In Hermann's white male imaginary, Canada and Australia both represent wild frontiers where he could go off on an adventure and make his own way.

While Hermann is away, he sends Maria a single rose every month, and she collects them all in a vase. This perhaps echoes the moment when Maria came to pick him up on the day of his release, carrying a single rose. From that day onward, though she is clearly disappointed by Hermann's letter about his emigration, Maria throws herself back into her work. She becomes increasingly unhappy with each passing day, drinking more and yelling at her secretary, Frau Emke (played by Fassbinder's mother). Maria's mother criticizes her, saying that she is wasting away waiting for Hermann. She says that it is as if Maria is slowly dying with each rose she that receives. Neither her work nor her relationship with Oswald seems to make her happy anymore.

The vase in which Maria keeps the roses that Hermann sends her will become an important part of the mise-en-scène when the two are reunited. In an earlier scene, after Maria gets home from talking with Willi about the union's negotiations with Oswald's company, she accidentally puts her purse into the vase instead of the rose that she has just received from Hermann, which she is holding in her other hand; this is a hint that her wealth is getting in the way of romance (Fig. 38). It also conveys a certain absent-mindedness that makes the cause of the deadly explosion at the end of the film ambiguous: is it an accident or not? In the same scene (Fig. 39), we also see that she likes to light her cigarette from the stove, which makes it more plausible that the explosion could be accidental.

In one of the final scenes of the movie, following his funeral, Maria dines at her and Oswald's favorite restaurant. The live broadcast of

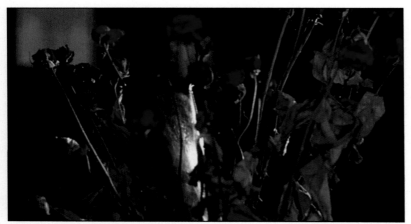

Figure 38. A close-up of the vase containing all of the roses Hermann has sent, in which Maria mistakenly placed her purse.

the 1954 soccer World Cup final that is playing at the restaurant acoustically links that scene with the next one, Hermann and Maria's reunion. According to Joyce Rheuban, it was Fassbinder who added the "ironic commentary" of the broadcast to the shooting script.[132] Back at Maria's house, the script describes her as being asleep on her couch and startled by Hermann ringing the bell. However, the film differs from the script, showing her with her head down at a table in the kitchen. The house is littered with empty bottles, a reference to Maria's drinking problem and indicating that this is how she has been dealing with her grief. Things are awkward between Maria and Hermann. Maria seems to be inching toward him, only to retreat. She suggests that they go on a honeymoon, only to then say she can't leave for a few days because she has some things to take care of. But each time she disappoints him, she tries to console him again. This back-and-forth indicates that as much as Maria *thinks* she wants Hermann to step into the role of head of the household, she is having trouble relinquishing power. Later, Hermann's insecurities show when he belittles her when she boasts that she is going to be a rich

Figure 39. Maria uses the gas stove to light her cigarette.

woman after inheriting a lot of money. His response—"Anyone can inherit things"—downplays the fact that she has also invested years of work to create this life for him. During their conversation, we see a close-up of Maria leaning over the gas stove to light her cigarette, a habit we witnessed in a previous scene. Only this time, instead of turning off the gas, she merely blows out the flame. And though Maria then straightens up and walks away, the camera lingers on the stove, with the leftmost knob still turned on partway (Fig. 40). We hear a faint sound of gas escaping into the room.

When the two finally attempt to be intimate, they are interrupted by the doorbell—it's Oswald's bookkeeper, Senkenberg, accompanied by a Ms. Delvaux, there to read the will. Maria rushes upstairs to change, so she doesn't hear all of the details of the will. She rushes back down the stairs just in time to hear that Oswald has left half of his assets to her. Ms. Delvaux reads: "The other half of the estate, as per our contract, signed at Kreuzhof Prison on the fourteenth day of June, 1951, shall go to Hermann Braun, who was a friend to me, even though he loved the same woman I did." It turns

Figure 40. A close-up of the stove after Maria blows out the flame.

out that Senkenberg had known about this contract. The only one who was in the dark about it was Maria, who suddenly announces that she has a headache and leaves the room. Her headache could either be a psychosomatic response to hearing the will read out or a reaction to the gas she has been breathing in since she failed to turn off the stove.

The film then cuts to an extreme close-up of Maria running water over her wrist as a cure for her headache (Fig. 41). But this image may also foreshadow a suicide. By the time Maria returns, Senkenberg and Delvaux have already left. Maria walks over to the vase of dried roses and removes a cigarette from a pack. The commodity that used to be so hard to come by is now as easy to get as anything else, thanks to Germany's economic recovery and her own financial success. Hermann tries to make her feel better about his deception, stressing that he doesn't care about the money, he'll give it all to her anyway. Her response, "I've given you everything too," makes it clear that she is not just talking about money, but about her whole life.[133] Maria asks Hermann for a light, only to immediately walk towards the

Figure 41. An extreme close-up of Maria with her head down at the sink.

stove, presumably to light her cigarette herself. Once Maria walks out of the frame, we never see her again. All we see is Hermann, sitting on the bed facing a glass door, with his back to the camera. He sits with his head down. Suddenly, he turns around to look for her. Perhaps he smells the gas that has been leaking this entire time. He jumps off the bed yelling "No," covering his face.

We don't see the explosion, we just hear it. And we experience it from the perspective of Senkenberg and Delvaux, who are walking away from the house when it happens. As soon as the explosion happens, the film's title blends in again, once again in red lettering, mirroring the beginning and bringing the film full circle (Fig. 42). Senkenberg and Delvaux turn around to see the house on fire; he returns to check on Maria. Her and Hermann's deaths are confirmed when we witness Senkenberg's reaction as he looks down at them. We don't actually see Maria, we just see Hermann's arm with his gold watch. The explosion has thrown bedding everywhere and done much the same to the roses. The phone is on the floor, with the receiver off the hook. Its dial tone keeps sounding until the very end

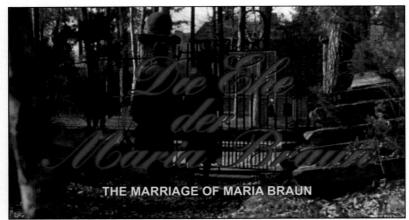

Figure 42. The film's title blends in, as Senkenberg and Ms. Delvaux walk away at the moment of the explosion.

of the film. As we view this chaotic scene, in the background we hear the soccer commentator Zimmermann announce on the radio broadcast: "It's over! It's over!"

When people asked Fassbinder whether the ending of the film indicates suicide or an accident and why he chose to leave things so ambivalent, his response was that "Ms. Schygulla didn't want to die in the film," indicating that it was her star power, her ego, that influenced him.[134] Schygulla, however, has described the film's ending this way: "The story of Maria Braun ends with a bang, during which her strained existence dissolves."[135]

After the shot of Hermann lying dead, the screen fades to white, and in the final seconds of the film, a series of negatives of past West German chancellors is blended in, all while the sound of the dial tone keeps repeating. We see Adenauer (Fig. 43), who served from 1949 to 1963, then Ludwig Erhard (1963–1966), Kurt Georg Kiesinger (1966–1969), and finally Helmut Schmidt (1974–1982). The only chancellor who is excluded is Willi Brandt, apparently because Fassbinder didn't associate him with the same authoritarianism as

Figure 43. A negative image of Konrad Adenauer, the first of a succession of West German chancellors shown.

the others. With this parade of past chancellors, mirroring the film's beginning with a portrait of Hitler, Fassbinder implies that one can see a direct link between the Nazi past and West Germany's political and social problems since.

Conclusion

Despite the success that *Maria Braun* brought Fassbinder both at home and abroad, it was not quite the international breakthrough he had hoped for. He had hoped *Maria Braun* would win him an Oscar, giving him the notoriety necessary for working in the American film industry. But Fassbinder didn't win an Oscar; that honor went to Volker Schlöndorff for *The Tin Drum*. And instead of Fassbinder, it was several other New German Cinema directors who would ultimately find fame working in America, for instance Werner Herzog and Wim Wenders.

More recently, *Maria Braun* has found an interesting afterlife on the theater stage, where, especially since the 2000s, it has been staged by numerous German, and some foreign, directors, from Munich to Berlin to Holland. One such director who has brought *Maria Braun* to the stage is Thomas Ostermeier, who directed a stage production of *Maria Braun* for the Münchener Kammerspiele, which was then later invited to the Theatertreffen in Berlin in 2008. The fact that Ostermeier cast a white actor to play Bill suggests that contemporary audiences still haven't problematized the racist legacy of German theater, let alone Maria's instrumentalization of Black men. Truly coming to terms with how Black men are portrayed in *Maria Braun* and how they are treated by the protagonist would also involve casting a Black man in the role of Bill. If Ostermeier were familiar with contemporary discussions around race and representation in German film and theater, he would be aware of Black Germans' concerns about how Blackness is portrayed in the German media. These concerns include worry about Black men's hypersexualization and objectification and the legacy of white women benefitting from racism, without being held accountable for their privilege. All of these issues can be addressed in a contemporary staging of *Maria Braun*, but certainly not when one of the only Black roles is given to a white actor.

Perhaps Ostermeier failed to think more critically about the role of race in *Maria Braun*, because although he sees the narrative as an interpretation of the "founding myth of the FRG," he doesn't see race as essential for understanding this myth.[136] According to Ostermeier, what went wrong with the FRG was that Germans substituted materialism "for religion, for the lost ideology [of the Nazi period] and a past that wasn't dealt with."[137] A key part of dealing with Nazi ideology is addressing racism as well as antisemitism; and this is an argument that activists and scholars continue to make vis a vis Germans' efforts to decolonize their thinking. However, even today, over forty years since *Maria Braun* was made, Germans still have trouble properly interrogating the anti-Black tendencies in their society.

In an interview, Fassbinder was asked whether he loved "failed people." Fassbinder responded:

> I have a tender feeling for them. I understand them in everything they did wrong. Maybe that has to do with myself, too. You always tell yourself—OK, you're not going to let yourself be ruined—but it can happen to me. There are already people waiting for me to collapse.[138]

In essence, the director and his protagonist had much in common. Their lives were a series of ups and downs, twists and turns, ending with the tragic death of someone who desperately wanted control, but never really had it. And Fassbinder and Maria share a character flaw as well: the tendency to exploit Black men. Although Fassbinder recognized this enough in Maria to highlight it in the film, from what we know about his life, he lacked a self-awareness of his own perpetuation of racism.

CREDITS

Director:
Rainer Werner Fassbinder

Writer:
Peter Märthesheimer and Pea Fröhlich,
  from an idea by Rainer Werner
  Fassbinder

Production Companies:
Albatros Filmproduktion
Fengler Films
Filmverlag der Autoren
Tango Film
Trio Film
Westdeutscher Rundfunk (WDR)

Produced by:
Michael Fengler
Wolf-Dietrich Brücker
Volker Canaris
Hanns Eckelkamp

Cast:
Hanna Schygulla (Maria)
Klaus Löwitsch (Hermann)
Ivan Desny (Oswald)
Gottfried John (Willi)
Gisela Uhlen (Mother)
Georg Byrd (Bill)
Elisabeth Trissenaar (Betti)
Hark Bohm (Senkenberg)
Günther Kaufman (Lonely Richard)

Music:
Peer Raben

Cinematography:
Michael Ballhaus

Film Editing:
Julia Lorenz
Franz Walsch [Rainer Werner Fassbinder]

Production Direction:
Martin Häussler

Costume Design:
Barbara Baum
Susi Riechel
Georg Hahn
Ingeberg Pröller

Running time:
120 min.

Sound Mix:
Mono

Color:
Color

Aspect Ratio:
1.66:1

Film Length:
3296 m

Negative Format:
35 mm

Cinematographic Process:
Spherical

Printed Film Format:
35 mm

Production Costs:
DM 1,975,000 (inflation
  adjusted ca. $ 2.4 Million
  in 2022)

Release Dates:
March 1979 (West Germany), May
  1979 (France), September 1979
  (Netherlands, Canada, Portugal),
  October 1979 (US, Finland)

NOTES

1 Rainer Werner Fassbinder, "Six Films by Douglas Sirk," in *The Marriage of Maria Braun*, ed. Joyce Rheuban (New Brunswick, NJ: Rutgers University Press, 1986), 205.

2 Fassbinder, "Six Films by Douglas Sirk," 206.

3 Thomas Schatz, *Hollywood Genres: Formulas, Filmmaking and the Studio System* (Boston, MA: McGraw-Hill, 1981), 225.

4 DFF—Deutsches Filminstitut & Filmmuseum, Frankfurt am Main/Fassbinder Handschriften-Archiv @ Juliane Marie Lorenz-Wehling/Rainer Werner Fassbinder Foundation, Akte 106.022 (1978), Inserat-Matern (37/1118).

5 Hanna Schygulla, *Hanna Schygulla: Bilder aus Filmen von Rainer Werner Fassbinder* (Munich: Scjirmer/Mosel, 1981), 35.

6 Deutsche Film- und Fernsehakademie Berlin, dffb (German Film and Television Academy Berlin), Akte 1797, Die Sehnsucht der Veronika Voss, "Gespräch mit Rainer Werner Fassbinder," 8. All translations from German to English are by the author.

7 Joyce Rheuban, "Notes on Shooting Script," in *The Marriage of Maria Braun*, ed. Rheuban, 179.

8 Rheuban, "Notes on Shooting Script," 153.

9 Peter W. Jansen, *"Die Zeit,"* in *The Marriage of Maria Braun*, ed. Rheuban, 221.

10 Ruth McCormick, *"Cineaste,"* in *The Marriage of Maria Braun*, ed. Rheuban, 225.

11 Fassbinder in a letter to Romy Schneider from June 28, 1975, DFF—Deutsches Filminstitut & Filmmuseum, Frankfurt am Main/Fassbinder Handschriften-Archiv @ Juliane Marie Lorenz-Wehling/Rainer Werner Fassbinder Foundation, Akte 106.032.

12 Hanna Schissler, "Normalization as Project: Some Thoughts on Gender Relations in West Germany During the 1950s," in *The Miracle Years: A Cultural History of West Germany 1949–1968*, ed. Hanna Schissler, (Princeton, NJ: Princeton University Press, 2001), 361.

13 Schissler, "Normalization as Project," 361.

14 Dagmar Herzog, *Sex After Fascism: Memory and Morality in Twentieth-Century Germany* (Princeton, NJ: Princeton University Press, 2005), 11.

15 Jürgen Trimborn, *Ein Tag ist ein Jahr ist ein Leben: Rainer Werner Fassbinder; Die Biografie* (Berlin: Ullstein, 2012), 14.

16 Interestingly, the choice Fassbinder's mother faced, between caring for him herself and leaving him with relatives so that she could work and help provide a better standard of life, is similar to the dilemma both women in *Imitation of Life* faced and about which I will say more in a later section.

17   Trimborn, *Ein Tag ist ein Jahr*, 16.

18   See Maria Höhn, *GIs and Fräuleins: The German-American Encounter in 1950s West Germany* (Chapel Hill: University of North Carolina Press, 2002). See also Annette Brauerhoch, *"Fräuleins" und GIs: Geschichte und Filmgeschichte* (Frankfurt am Main: Stroemfeld/Nexus, 2006).

19   Amy Rutenberg, "Service by Other Means: Changing Perceptions of Military Service and Masculinity in the United States, 1940–1973," in *Gender and the Long Postwar: The United States and the Two Germanys, 1945–1989*, ed. Karen Hagemann and Sonya Michel (Baltimore, MD: Johns Hopkins University Press, 2014), 189.

20   Timothy Schroer, *Recasting Race after WWII: Germans and African Americans in American-Occupied Germany* (Boulder: University of Colorado Press, 2007), 83–84. Since prostitution was legal in West Germany at this time, officials could only use the German Criminal Code (§361 No. 6a-c) to "indict prostitutes for transgressing certain boundaries" (Höhn, *GIs and Fräuleins*, 154). Furthermore, as Maria Höhn writes, in small towns it was relatively easy to control the women suspected of being prostitutes: "As soon as a single woman was observed in a pub or bar where American soldiers congregated, her identification papers were checked by the police officers, who patrolled these bars every night at regular intervals" (200). If a woman didn't have an ID, she could be jailed.

21   dffb, Akte 1797, Die Sehnsucht der Veronika Voss, "Gespräch mit Rainer Werner Fassbinder," 6.

22   Dagmar Herzog argues: "There was a distinctive force and fury to West German debates over sex and a heightened drama to the resulting social transformations. The new consensus developed in the early to mid-1960s by liberal intellectuals and New Left activists that the Third Reich had been not only brutally but also uniformly sexually repressive became so widely assumed as to seem incontrovertible." Herzog, *Sex After Fascism*, 141–42.

23   In 2009, researchers "looking into Berlin Wall deaths and East German intelligence" found that the policeman who shot Ohnesorg, Karl-Heins Kurras, had in fact been an East German "Stasi" spy embedded within the West Berlin police. Nicholas Kulish, "Spy Fired Shot That Changed West Germany," *New York Times*, May 26, 2009, https://www.nytimes.com/2009/05/27/world/europe/27germany.html.

24   Alexander and Margarete Mitscherlich, *The Inability to Mourn* (New York: Grove Press, 1975), 4.

25   Mitscherlich and Mitscherlich, *The Inability to Mourn*, 13–14.

26   See Thomas Elsaesser, *Fassbinder's Germany: History, Identity, Subject* (Amsterdam: Amsterdam University Press, 1996).

27   Linda Williams, *Playing the Race Card: Melodramas of Black and White from Uncle Tom to O. J. Simpson* (Princeton, NJ: Princeton University Press, 2001), 6.

28   Schatz, *Hollywood Genres*, 222.

29 John Mercer and Martin Shingler, *Melodrama: Genre, Style and Sensibility* (London: Columbia University Press, 2013), 10.

30 The film cost 1.95 million DM to produce, which at the time was the equivalent of $940,000. Thus, although earning $1 million in one year may not seem significant, it still meant the production costs were covered, leaving a profit of $60,000.

31 Homi Bhabha, "The Other Question. . .," *Screen* 24, no. 6 (1983): 18.

32 See Kara Keeling, *The Witch's Flight: The Cinematic, the Black Femme, and the Image of Common Sense* (Durham, NC: Duke University Press, 2007).

33 See Eric Lott, *Love and Theft: Blackface Minstrelsy and the American Working Class* (New York: Oxford University Press, 1993); and Michael Rogin, *Blackface, White Noise: Jewish Immigrants in the Hollywood Melting Pot* (Berkeley: University of California Press, 1996).

34 Williams, *Playing the Race Card*, 6.

35 Williams, *Playing the Race Card*, 98.

36 Mercer and Shingler, *Melodrama*, 71.

37 Sirk was born Hans Detlef Sierck to Danish parents in Hamburg in 1900. He didn't change his name to Douglas Sirk until he arrived in the US in the early 1940s. In Germany, Sirk first worked as a stage director before making films for UFA (Universum Film-Aktien Gesellschaft), a German film and television production company that operated from 1917 until the end of World War II.

38 Anton Kaes, *From Hitler to Heimat: The Return of History as Film* (Cambridge, MA: Harvard University Press, 1989), 78.

39 Fassbinder, "Six Films by Douglas Sirk," 205.

40 Cerise L. Glenn, "'The Power of Black Magic': The Magical Negro and White Salvation in Film," *Journal of Black Studies* 40, no. 2 (2009): 135.

41 Remarque's novel, written in German as *Zeit zu leben und Zeit zu sterben* (Time to Live and Time to Die), was published in English translation in 1954, almost simultaneously with the German original. Remarque fled Nazi Germany in 1938, but his work had begun to come under attack long before that. His books were being burned as early as 1933, when Hitler seized power, and the Nazi protests against his book *Im Westen nichts Neues* (1928; *All Quiet on the Western Front*, 1929) even predated the National Socialist regime. In 1947, Remarque and his wife became naturalized American citizens.

42 In the exposé written before the script, the baby does not die. Rather, Maria goes into labor while Hermann stands trial for Bill's murder and she gives birth to a "strong and healthy, but colored child . . ., who is given the name Ronald at baptism and is taken by Maria to be cared for in the country, where her mother's sister runs a small shop in a village near the city." The fact that Fassbinder ultimately chose for the child *not* to survive emphasizes that Maria had to either choose herself *or* being a mother. In the exposé, not only does Maria have a secret child, but she also becomes pregnant with

Oswald's child. The conflict of Maria's marriage to Hermann and her secret child is resolved when she confesses it all to Oswald and he not only decides to stay with Maria, but also adopts her older child. Thus, while Fassbinder initially envisioned for Maria to have a happy ending, married to Oswald with two children, it is significant that he instead chose a very different path for her in the film.

43 Fassbinder, "Six Films," 204–5.

44 Originally, *Maria Braun* was supposed to contains scenes of Hermann in a Soviet prisoner of war camp, but Fassbinder decided against it. See Rheuban, "Notes on Shooting Script," 164.

45 Gerald Peary, "Rated GP: What's All Der Führer About," *The Real Paper Boston*, November 24, 1979.

46 Kaes, *From Hitler to Heimat*, 78.

47 Schatz, *Hollywood Genres*, 222.

48 Schatz, *Hollywood Genres*, 222.

49 Lauren Berlant, *Cruel Optimism* (Durham, NC: Duke University Press, 2011), 24.

50 Norbert Sparrow, "Ich lasse die Zuschauer fühlen und denken" [1977], in *Fassbinder über Fassbinder: Die ungekürzten Interviews*, ed. Robert Fischer (Frankfurt am Main: Verlag der Autoren, 2004), 406.

51 Johannes von Moltke, "Camping in the Art Closet: The Politics of Camp and Nation in German Film," *New German Critique* 63 (1994): 98–99.

52 Michael Sragow, "A shy domestic flower who blooms into a Venus' flytrap," *Los Angeles Herald Examiner*, November 18, 1979.

53 Rheuban, "Notes on Shooting Script," 165.

54 "Heinrich von Kleist in den Fängen der Nazis," *Die Tageszeitung*, August 5, 2008, https://taz.de/Heinrich-von-Kleist-in-den-Faengen-der-Nazis/!833374/.

55 Tom Reiss, "How the Nazis Created a Dream Factory in Hell," *New York Times*, November 6, 1994, https://www.nytimes.com/1994/11/06/movies/film-how-the-nazis-created-a-dream-factory-in-hell.html.

56 Fassbinder got his directorial start in the Anti-Theater, previously Action-Theater, in Munich. At the time, Fassbinder was attending the Fridl-Leonhard acting school, roughly from 1964 to 1966. That's where he met the actresses Schuygulla and Marite Greiselis. It was Greiselis who would introduce him to the Action-Theater. She had a role in Raben's production of *Antigone*, which she invited Fassbinder to view. Fassbinder was fascinated by the production and returned several more times "and was asked to stand in for one of the actors . . . who had accidentally injured himself." This would be Fassbinder's opportunity to gain more influence in the theater, first by becoming a full member of the group, then persuading them to stop hiring hippies and instead engage serious actors, and finally directing plays. David Barnett, *Rainer Werner Fassbinder and the German Theatre* (Cambridge: Cambridge University Press, 2005), 32.

57 This match was so significant because the German national team's win over Hungary gave West Germans the first chance to feel a sense of national pride since the nation's founding in 1945. Prior to that, West Germans had not felt comfortable exhibiting pride, as they spent their postwar years atoning for the crimes of the Second World War and struggling to find economic stability. This World Cup win was a huge boost for national pride and is known as "Das Wunder von Bern" (the Miracle of Bern), portrayed in greater detail in a film by the same name, directed by Sönke Wortmann.

58 Joyce Rheuban, "*The Marriage of Maria Braun*: History, Melodrama, Ideology," in *The Marriage of Maria Braun*, ed. Rheuban, 4.

59 Wolfgang Gast, "Erinnerungsbilder der 50er Jahre im Film: Montage und Bildkom position als filmsprachliche Referenzmittel am Beispiel von Edgar Reitz' *1. Heimat* (1984), Rainer Werner Fassbinders *BRD-Trilogie* (1978–1981) und Sönke Wortmanns *Das Wunder von Bern* (2003)," in *Das "Prinzip Erinnerung" in der deutschsprachigen Gegenwartsliteratur nach 1989*, ed. Carsten Gansel and Pawel Zimniak (Göttingen: V&R Unipress, 2010), 349.

60 Rheuban, "Notes on Shooting Script," 165.

61 Rheuban, "Notes on Shooting Script," 165.

62 According to Alice Kuzinar, both Leander and Marlene Dietrich appealed to gay men because their performances often depended on gender as a construct. Both actresses blurred the categories of masculine and feminine; Dietrich in her cross-dressing attire and Leander with her baritone voice. And both actresses became specters, with whom gay male viewers could identify, because their roles so often played with illusion, glamour, and the hope that there could be a more ideal world for marginalized people. Alice Kuzniar, *The Queer German Cinema* (Stanford, CA: Stanford University Press, 2000), 30–35 and 62–65. In a film review entitled "Zarah Leander and Transgender Specularity," Kuzniar also cites queer director Rosa von Praunheim (b. 1942) who says of Leander: "When in her films Zarah sang with tears in her eyes, vulnerable yet mastering her misfortune, and thundering out against it 'Kann denn Liebe Sünde sein?' [Can Love Be a Sin?] you just had to lie down and identify with her." Alice Kuzniar, "Zarah Leander and Transgender Specularity," *Film Criticism* 23, no. 2/3 (1999): 74.

63 Ulrike Sieglohr, *Hanna Schygulla* (London: BFI, 2014), 40.

64 Erica Carter, *Dietrich's Ghosts: The Sublime and the Beautiful in Third Reich Film* (London: BFI, 2004), 212.

65 Rebecca Behling, "Gender Roles in Ruins: German Women and Local Politics under American Occupation, 1945–1955," in *Gender and the Long Postwar*, ed. Hagemann and Michel, 51.

66 Höhn, *GIs and Fräuleins*, 21.

67 Gerd Gemünden, *A Foreign Affair: Billy Wilder's American Films* (New York: Berghahn, 2008), 69.

68 For a detailed analysis of *A Foreign Affair*, see Gemünden, *A Foreign Affair*, 54–75; and

Gerd Gemünden, *Continental Strangers: German Exile Cinema* (New York: Columbia University Press, 2014).

69   See Höhn, *GIs and Fräuleins*; and Annette Brauerhoch, *"Fräuleins" und Gis: Geschichte und Filmgeschichte* (Frankfurt am Main: Stroemfeld/Nexus, 2006).

70   Susan L. Carruthers, *The Good Occupation: American Soldiers and the Hazards of Peace* (Cambridge, MA: Harvard University Press, 2016), 63.

71   Rainer Werner Fassbinder and Kurt Raab, "Die Männer der Maria Braun. Exposé für einen Spielfilm von Rainer Werner Fassbinder und Kurt Raab," Fassbinder Archive, Akte 106.001, 58.

72   "The Continuity Script," in *The Marriage of Maria Braun*, ed. Rheuban, 41.

73   Moritz Ege, Andrew Wright Hurley, and Sydney Portal, "Periodizing and Historicizing German Afro-Americanophilia: From Antebellum to Postwar (1850–1965)," *PORTAL* 12, no. 2 (2015): 19. See also Raymond M. Weinstein, "Occupation G.I. Blues: Postwar Germany During and After Elvis Presley's Tour," *Popular Culture* 39, no. 1 (2006): 126–49.

74   Schroer, *Recasting Race*, 28.

75   75 Schroer, *Recasting Race*, 28.

76   Maria Höhn and Martin Klimke, *A Breath of Freedom: The Civil Rights Struggle, African American GIs, and Germany* (New York: Palgrave Macmillan, 2010), 39.

77   See Michael J. Budds, *Jazz and the Germans: Essays on the Influence of "Hot" American Idioms on 20th-Century German Music* (Hillsdale, NY: Pendragon Press, 2002).

78   Caroline Drees, "Finally, Glenn Miller's Propaganda Serenade," *The Seattle Times*, February 13, 1995.

79   Drees, "Finally, Glenn Miller's Propaganda Serenade."

80   Höhn, *GIs and Fräuleins*, 24. See also Ute G. Poiger, *Jazz, Rock, and Rebels: Cold War Politics and American Culture in a Divided Germany* (Berkeley: University of California, 2000).

81   Jean-Denis Lepage, *Hitler's Stormtroopers: The SA, the Nazis' Brownshirts, 1922–1945* (Barnsley: Pen & Sword Books, 2016), xiii.

82   Katrin Sieg refers to "ethnic drag" as "not only cross-racial casting on the stage, but more generally, the performance of 'race' as a masquerade.... Ethnic drag reveals ... the continuities, permutations, and contradictions of racial feelings in West German culture." Katrin Sieg, *Ethnic Drag* (Ann Arbor: University of Michigan Press, 2002), 2.

83   dffb, Folder 4.4—1983/12.89, Die Ehe der Maria Braun.

84   dffb, Folder 4.4—1983/12.89, Die Ehe der Maria Braun.

85   Rheuban, "Notes on Shooting Script," 166.

86   Volker Baer, "Die Ehe der Maria Braun," *Tagesspiegel*, February 21, 1979.

87   Jeffrey Lyon, Radio TV Report, *Newsradio 88*, November 19, 1979, 12:21 p.m., New York.

88   Fassbinder and Raab, "Die Männer der Maria Braun," 4.

89   ". . . not even during her affair with a black American soldier who makes her pregnant—does she stop loving her husband or considering herself still married to him." Constance Gorfinkle, "'Maria Braun'—charming blend of allegory, humor, melodrama," *The Patriot Ledger Boston*, September 20, 2001.

90   See Fatima El-Tayeb, *Schwarze Deutsche: Der Diskurs um "Rasse" und nationale Identität 1890–1933* (Frankfurt and New York: Campus, 2001); Katharina Oguntoye, *Eine afro-deutsche Geschichte: Zur Lebenssituation von Afrikanern und Afro-Deutschen in Deutschland von 1884 bis 1950* (Berlin: Hoho Verlag Christine Hoffmann, 1997); Tina Campt, *Other Germans: Black Germans and the Politics of Race, Gender, and Memory in the Third Reich* (Ann Arbor: University of Michigan Press, 2004); and Iris Wigger, *"Die Schwarze Schmach am Rhein": rassistische Diskriminierung zwischen Geschlecht, Klasse, Nation und Rasse* (Münster: Westfälisches Dampfboot, 2007).

91   Julia Roos remarks that one can find "discourses blaming Germany's defeat on women's 'promiscuity,'" and she cites an example from "a complaint voiced by Aachen's police commissioner during January 1920." Julia Ross, "Women's Rights, Nationalist Anxiety, and the 'Moral' Agenda in the Early Weimar Republic: Revisiting the 'Black Horror' Campaign against France's African Occupation Troops," *Central European History* 42, no. 3 (2009): 484.

92   Ingeborg Majer O'Sickey, "Representing Blackness: Instrumentalizing Race and Gender in Rainer Werner Fassbinder's *The Marriage of Maria Braun*," *Women in German Yearbook* 17 (2001): 20.

93   Tobias Nagl and Janelle Blankenship examine Blackness in Fassbinder's work as it pertains to Kaufmann and the possibility for individual black stardom in Germany in "'So Much Tenderness': Rainer Werner Fassbinder, Günther Kaufmann, and the Ambivalences of Interracial Desire," in *A Companion to Rainer Werner Fassbinder*, ed. Brigitte Peucker (Malden, MA: Wiley-Blackwell, 2012), 516–641.

94   Wallace Steadman Watson refers to Kaufmann as Fassbinder's lover at the time of shooting. According to Watson, Kaufmann then ended his relationship with Fassbinder and became involved with Peer Raben. See Wallace Steadman Watson, *Understanding Rainer Werner Fassbinder: Film as Private and Public Art* (Columbia: University of South Carolina Press, 1996), 85, 94. Christian Braad Thomsen also claims that Kaufman was Fassbinder's lover and that *The Bitter Tears of Petra von Kant*, a story about a lesbian couple, drew on Fassbinder's relationship with Kaufmann. Christian Braad Thomsen, *Fassbinder: The Life and Work of a Provocative Genius* (London and Boston, MA: Faber and Faber, 1997), 20.

95   Thomsen, *Fassbinder: The Life and Work of a Provocative Genius*, 20–21.

96   Nagl and Blankenship, "So Much Tenderness," 519.

97 Jürgen Trimmborn, *Ein Tag ist ein Jahr ist ein Leben: Rainer Werner Fassbinder; Die Biographie* (Berlin: Ullstein, 2012), 331.

98 DFF—Deutsches Filminstitut & Filmmuseum, Frankfurt am Main/Fassbinder Handschriften-Archiv @ Juliane Marie Lorenz-Wehling/Rainer Werner Fassbinder Foundation, Inserat-Matern (37/1118).

99 See Kira Thurman, *Singing Like Germans: Black Musicians in the Land of Bach, Beethoven and Brahms* (Ithaca, NY: Cornell University Press, 2021).

100 Allen Hughes, "And Now There are Three," *New York Times*, March 17, 1968.

101 D. A. Handy, *Black Conductors* (Metuchen, NJ: Scarecrow Press), 486.

102 Raymond Ericson, "More Deserving Than Panthers?," *New York Times*, October 29, 1972.

103 Ericson, "More Deserving Than Panthers?"

104 DFF—Deutsches Filminstitut & Filmmuseum, Frankfurt am Main/Fassbinder Handschriften-Archiv @ Juliane Marie Lorenz-Wehling/Rainer Werner Fassbinder Foundation, 106.031 Darstellerliste und Stabliste (1978).

105 Author interview with Sonja Spirk, November 16, 2021.

106 On the IMDB page for *The Marriage of Maria Braun*, Byrd is also credited as George Eagles and his role is described as "Bill (as George Byrd)."

107 Author interview with Sonja Spirk.

108 Drees, "Finally, Glenn Miller's Propaganda Serenade."

109 Fassbinder and Raab, "Die Männer der Maria Braun," 3.

110 Laura Mulvey, "Visual Pleasure and Narrative Cinema," *Screen* 16, no. 3 (1975): 808–9.

111 Karena Niehoff, "Eisblume, eingefroren für den großen Tag," *Süddeutsche Zeitung*, February 23, 1979.

112 Kathleen J. Reich, "Racially Mixed Marriages in Colonial Namibia," in *Crosscurrents: African Americans, Africa, and Germany in the Modern World*, ed. David McBride, Leroy Hopkins, and Carol Blackshire-Belay (Columbia, SC: Camden House, 1998), 160.

113 Adolf Hitler, *Mein Kampf*, trans. Ralph Manheim (Boston, MA: Houghton Mifflin, 1971), 325.

114 O'Sickey, "Representing Blackness," 17.

115 Heide Fehrenbach, *Race after Hitler: Black Occupation Children in Postwar Germany and America* (Princeton, NJ: Princeton University Press, 2005), 74.

116 See Oguntoye, *Eine afro-deutsche Geschichte*; and David Okuefuna's 1997 film, *Hitler's Forgotten Victims: Black Survivors of the Holocaust*.

117 Heide Fehrenbach, "Black Occupation Children and the Devolution of the Nazi Racial State," in *After the Nazi Racial State*, ed. Rita Chin, Heide Fehrenbach, Geoff Eley, and Atina Grossmann (Ann Arbor: University of Michigan Press, 2009), 44.

118 Fehrenbach, "Black Occupation Children," 44.

119 See Yara-Collette Lemke Muniz de Faria, *Zwischen Fürsorge und Ausgrenzung: Afrodeutsche "Besatzungskinder" im Nachkriegsdeutschland* (Berlin: Metropol, 2002); and Fehrenbach, *Race after Hitler*.

120 Fehrenbach, *Race after Hitler*, 133.

121 Niehoff, "Eisblume, eingefroren für den großen Tag."

122 Kaes, *From Hitler to Heimat*, 83.

123 Kaes, *From Hitler to Heimat*, 85.

124 dffb, Folder 4.4—1983/12.89, Die Ehe der Maria Braun, 49.

125 Elsaesser, *Fassbinder's Germany*, 114.

126 dffb, Folder 4.4—1983/12.89, Die Ehe der Maria Braun, 52.

127 Rainer Werner Fassbinder, "Imitation of Life," in *Imitation of Life*, ed. Lucy Fischer (Rutgers, NJ: Rutgers University Press, 1991), 244.

128 According to a theater script for *Maria Braun*, Maria miscarries and goes to the doctor for aftercare. However, in the film it is not clearly stated whether she miscarries or has an abortion. Fassbinder Archive, 106.022 (1978), 19; 106.029.

129 129 Nagl and Blankenship, "So Much Tenderness," 533; and Richard Combs, "Marriage of Maria Braun, The (Die Ehe der Maria Braun)," *Monthly Film Bulletin* 47, no. 552 (1980): 155.

130 O'Sickey, "Race and Gender," 20.

131 In the shooting script, Maria does tell Oswald about her husband. Rheuban, "Notes on Shooting Script," 177.

132 Rheuban, "Notes on Shooting Script," 178.

133 In the shooting script, this is the line Maria says right before she drives them over the embankment.

134 Rheuban, "Notes on Shooting Script," 178.

135 Schygulla, *Hanna Schygulla: Bilder aus Filmen von Rainer Werner Fassbinder*, 34.

136 Hermann Weiß, "Prototyp einer starken Frau; Zum 25. Todestag des Münchner Filmemachers Rainer Werner Fassbinder kommt einer seiner größten Kinoerfolge ins Theater. Thomas Ostermeier inszeniert 'Die Ehe der Maria Braun' an den Kammerspielen," *Die Welt am Sonntag*, June 3, 2007.

137 Weiß, "Prototyp einer starken Frau."

138 dffb, Akte 1797, Die Sehnsucht der Veronika Voss, "Gespräch mit Rainer Werner Fassbinder," 7.

Printed in the United States
by Baker & Taylor Publisher Services